Kona Secrets

ROB CUMMINS

About the author

Rob is a former smoker who only just made it into the top 1000 at his first two Ironman races. His third attempt was the charm though and saw him finish 26th in the amateur pool, missing out on qualifying for the Ironman World Championships in Kona by two minutes and one place. Rob now has sixteen Ironman races under his belt and has raced in Kona twice.

When they are not running triathlons, Rob and his wife Aisling run Wheelworx, the biggest specialist triathlon and run shop in Dublin, Ireland and an Ironman coaching company together. They have three dogs, no cats, too many bikes to count and can be found most days swimming, biking or running somewhere around Dublin.

Also by Rob Cummins

Chasing Kona: From Smoker to the Ironman World Championships

Available from Amazon in paperback or ebook here

Acknowledgments/contributions

A number of people very kindly contributed to and helped me with this project. First and foremost is Aisling. Ais was the was the one who believed that I could qualify for Kona even before I did myself. I couldn't train as I do without her help, guidance, coaching and support.

As well as basing this book on the lessons I learnt about going from the back of the pack to Kona, I also spoke to a number of athletes who had made the same journey themselves. This included everybody from first-timers to multiple Kona qualifiers, as well as a winner of the overall amateur race in Kona and professional athletes. There were many similarities in their comments but there were also some interesting differences in ideas, approaches and what worked for each of them. These amazing people helped me along the way, let me in on some of their secrets, tips and training sessions and were very generous with their time.

The professionals

Jocelyn Gardner McCauley

Aisling and I were at the awards ceremony for Ironman Mallorca in 2016. We were sitting in the sunshine on the beach waiting for the proceedings to start when an athlete asked if the chair next to us was free. She sat down and we chatted to her about how her race went and she asked about ours.

When the ceremony was underway and Paul Kaye, the voice of Ironman in Europe and Africa came to announce the female podium places, he called Jocelyn Gardner McCauley, the winner of the women's race, up to the stage. The woman sitting beside us stood up grinning and headed onto the stage beside Paul and took her place on the top step on the podium. We were suitably impressed, not only because she had won the race but because of how humble and gracious she was when we talked to her and posed for pictures with her and her trophy.

Jocelyn qualified for Kona at her first attempt as an age group athlete and then went on to win the overall amateur race in Kona, also at her first attempt. As a professional, she has won several Ironman events and in 2017 finished in the top ten in Kona. She was very generous with her time when I contacted her for assistance with this book and immediately agreed to help before she even knew what would be involved.

Emma Bilham

I met Emma on a training camp in Lanzarote but had read about her previously when Brett Sutton, the most successful triathlon coach in the world, christened her the 'Little Cabbage'. I had also read some of her blogs and followed her racing.

Emma raced short course International Triathlon Union (ITU) before switching to middle and long distance non-drafting racing where she found immediate success at middle distance. She also discovered her talent for Ironman when she raced three full distance events in the summer of 2016, placing second in her first two and fourth in the famous Embrunman long distance triathlon in the French Alps. Emma has been just as generous and helpful with her time helping me with this project.

The media stars

John Newsom and Bevan James Eyles

I first came across John and Bevan's IMTalk podcast back in 2007 when I was getting set to do my first Ironman. It's funny, but when you go around with someone talking inside your head for close to a dozen years you feel like you know them. I met the lads in Kona in 2012 and reached out to them for their help with the book and like almost everyone I contacted, they too immediately agreed to help.

John raced triathlon as a professional and does so now as an elite age grouper. Both him and Bevan have qualified for, and raced in, Kona. John is a triathlon coach and a race organiser and Bevan is a coach and gym instructor. When you add in the fact that they host one of the longest-running and biggest Ironman and triathlon podcasts, they are both completely immersed in the sport.

The age groupers

Garron Mosley

Garron has turned himself into a perfectly rounded triathlete, seemingly without a weak sport, and with a confidence in his racing ability that is very impressive. With several Kona qualifications and two appearances on the Big Island so far (the second of which gave him a top ten age group finish), Garron has a unique and interesting view on getting to, and racing at, Kona.

Pragmatic, consistent and hardworking, he will tell you that there aren't any secrets to success; however, he does dispute the idea that you need to be clocking massive hours every week to get there. He maintains that quality over quantity is the key to his success.

Andy Kinnane

Andy is one of the first-time qualifiers I spoke to. Often the lessons we learn at our first qualification are very different to those we learn after racing Kona a half dozen times.

Emmet Kelly

Emmet is another first-time qualifier and an interesting example of how consistent training can lead to constant improvement. As a kid, Emmet ran to and from school every day, clocking miles and adding hours towards the 10,000 we are told it takes to become really elite at something. He was running and training consistently before a lot of us ever considered becoming athletes and so has a lot to offer.

Alan Ryan

Alan is a really good friend of mine who achieved five Kona qualifications and three appearances there. He finished two of those Kona races on the podium and has a unique insight into what's required to not only get to Kona, but to perform at the highest level once there.

Kevin Gilleece

Kevin has qualified for Kona twice and is a good example of someone who just gets a lot of consistently hard work done. I've been racing against Kevin for years on the local Irish race scene and have watched him turn his run into something of a weapon. He now regularly runs low or sub three-hour marathons at the back end of an Ironman.

Table of Contents

CHAPTER 1

Who am I, to write a book about getting to Kona?

Ever since I first saw Ironman Hawaii on TV in my early twenties, as a heavy smoker, I dreamed about racing there. It was only in 2011, when I asked Aisling (who's now my wife) if she thought it was realistic. She surprised me a little when she immediately said yes. I was surprised because I'd already competed in two Ironman events that didn't go so well. The first was Ironman France in Nice in 2008, where I finished just inside the top 1000. The second was in the following year, when I spent a solid six months training my skinny little arse off with the very secret intention of seeing how close I could get to one of those magical Kona slots. That July, I stood on the start line of my second Ironman in Switzerland. After all my hard work I moved up a grand total of about fifty places. I think the universe was telling me I wasn't Kona material. In fact, I wasn't even close.

Still, despite the apparent reality that I was slow, I'd spend my long training rides daydreaming about racing in Hawaii and telling myself that if I just focused on each sport individually then I wasn't a million miles away from hitting

would need to qualify. I reasoned that I was on

minutes away from where I'd need to be in the

ridden close to six hours in Nice, which is a mo

route. That somehow made me think that a five-

bike split was within my reach. Funny logic, I l

was how I saw it then.

The marathon, however, was another matter entil

I'd clocked a less than impressive four-and-a-half-hour

marathon on a pancake flat course, albeit in thirty-five-degree

heat. In Switzerland, I just about broke four hours. Again, it was

on a fairly flat course but in much cooler conditions. I knew

that I would need to run a substantially sub-three-and-a-half-

hour marathon to secure a Kona slot and, even if I could, it

would have to come off the back of a five-hour bike ride and a

sixty-five minute swim.

Despite my apparent lack of physical ability, Aisling saw some

potential that no one else (myself included) could see. Even

when she said that she thought I could succeed and that I should

have a go at chasing a Kona slot, I didn't really believe that I had

what it took. I wanted it and I wanted to believe it, but it really

felt like more of a dream than a possibility. But I trusted in

Aisling's belief in me and her judgement. So, we decided to have

a go.

We are both fairly impatient people and, in the beginning, we set a very short timescale in which to qualify. We thought: why aim to achieve something in twenty-four months if we could possibly achieve it in twelve instead? We knew that it might take considerably longer, but we didn't really look past that initial short-term goal because I wanted the pressure of the short timescale to keep me working hard and motivated to do things I had never thought physically possible. That doesn't mean that if we weren't successful then we would accept defeat and quit, if it took longer than twelve months we would, of course, keep on trying.

I think we have a unique perspective on what is required for an average athlete to make it to Kona: I didn't have a traditional or typical entry into the sport and I also didn't show any signs that I could race at the level that I eventually achieved. I didn't have what most people would have thought was required and I certainly didn't have any 'God-given talent'. If Olympic champion Usain Bolt won the genetic lottery then I won the equivalent of a local school raffle.

I started my athletic journey in my late twenties after more than a dozen years spent chain smoking, drinking and living a very unhealthy and sedentary lifestyle, before turning my life around. Up to the point that I stopped smoking I had never taken part in sport of any description outside of what I did in school physical education classes once a week for an hour, and that was only until I was sixteen (and, if I'm really honest with myself, most of those classes were spent trying to do as little as possible).

When I did stop smoking in 1999, I bought my first mountain bike as an incentive to keep it up. I couldn't ride for more than twenty minutes without needing to stop and rest but later that year decided to enter a race. As I rolled in dead last, I thought that it was the stupidest thing I had ever done and swore to myself that I would never do it again.

It didn't take long to be lured back in to try another race. It was funny how the misery and suffering of that first race was forgotten almost as soon as I got off the bike and was quickly replaced with the satisfaction of finishing something that I had thought was beyond me.

Over the next couple of years, I stuck with cycling and managed to move up from coming last place at my first race to being a consistent mid-pack finisher. But I always thought that those racers finishing at the front were a different species. I believed that they had that 'God-given talent' that I lacked. Back then I didn't know that the difference between the majority of those athletes and me was the number of hours in the saddle and lots of hard, consistent training.

I gradually moved towards road bike racing over the next few years, mostly out of convenience. I didn't have to drive to and from the trails like I did with mountain biking, I just walked out my front door and I was ready to ride. Unfortunately, road racing didn't reveal any hidden talent either. Over a couple of seasons I managed to become more competent and was able to finish near the front of a race, but I never realistically challenged for a win. My highest placing in a local club race was sixth.

This isn't a story about discovering the bike and cycling, and then finding out that I had a Ferrari engine lurking under the bonnet all that time. I looked at the guys winning my races and they were as far away from my reality as to be from a different planet; they were usually showered, dressed and eating lunch while I was still half a lap from the finish line. And I was only racing the entry-level Sport Category races. There were another two levels of freakishly talented athletes above me. And then there were the national and international level riders above them.

In 2003, I discovered triathlon and immediately fell in love with the sport, but I was back to being a beginner. I thought that because I had something of an engine built from a few years cycling I should do pretty well. I guess I did, on the bike leg at least. What I hadn't anticipated was that I would regularly be almost last out of the water and that I would spend the entire bike section chasing until I got to Transition 2 (T2) close to the top ten, at which point I was re-passed by most of the people I had caught on the bike.

It didn't matter that I was slow and finished at the back of the pack, what did matter was that I had found my sport and my passion, and so, over the next couple of seasons I became more and more involved in triathlon. After five years of triathlon, in 2008, I attempted my first Ironman.

It was while I was discovering Ironman that I met Aisling. She was a runner, a real runner who raced ultra-marathons and mountain races. Actually raced them, not just got around them like I did. And she won more often than not. She held course records in Irish mountain running races and, not long after I met her, she won a gold medal at the European Masters Mountain Running Championships in the summer of 2008.

Coincidentally, Aisling also did her first Ironman that year in the UK on the old Sherborne course, despite the fact that she couldn't swim a length of the pool only four months earlier. On race day she put her incredible running ability to good use as she ran the third fastest women's marathon of the day on her Ironman debut.

So, in 2011, when Aisling was telling me to try for Kona, I wanted so much to believe that she was right, but neither of us had a clue about how to go about it. Aisling was the one who suggested that we should get a coach and, as it happened, we knew someone who was coaching triathlon at the time and had raced as a professional Ironman triathlete for years. We reasoned that he would probably know what to do, so we approached him.

He didn't believe I was Kona material but, despite this, agreed to coach me like he would an actual Kona athlete. After working with him for the hardest five months of my life, I crossed the finish line of Ironman UK in thirty-sixth place. I beat some professionals in the process and finished eighth in my age group. I missed out on qualifying for Kona by only two minutes and one place and it had taken me less than six months to get to that stage. As an aside, Aisling also raced that Ironman and missed a Kona slot by only one place, and she wasn't even trying to qualify.

We left Bolton that year somewhat disappointed, but to be honest, my overriding feeling was of having achieved what we had set out to do. I now felt like a Kona athlete, even though I hadn't qualified. I was only two minutes away from a slot and, over a nine- or ten-hour race, I reasoned that two minutes was nothing. I felt that, as an athlete, I was already more or less there. I just had to execute properly on my next race day, and I did. I returned to Ironman UK for the following two years, qualified both times and raced in Kona in both 2012 and 2013.

I had worked with a couple of coaches before I asked Aisling to coach me in 2013. She had been coaching athletes for about 4 years for marathon, triathlon and Ironman. She agreed and still coaches me now. Over the past few years, Aisling's coaching roster grew and I became more involved to the point where I now coach alongside her.

This book is about the lessons we both learnt over the following three years, two Kona qualifications and the resulting two trips to the Big Island in Hawaii. It's also about the lessons Aisling and I have learnt in our seven years running a coaching business.

I got where I am by applying the biggest lesson I learnt from more than a dozen years spent working for myself: that hard work makes up for a lack of talent. I got here by consistently showing up and doing the work and not believing the people who told me it was impossible.

I've found that coaching and teaching athletes really made me examine what worked for me and why, so that I could in turn apply those principles and lessons to other athletes. I guess that's a big part of why I decided to write this book – to share the lessons that I learnt. Apart from that, I want to show that it is possible to do something that seems or looks impossible. I want to demonstrate that getting to Kona doesn't require winning the genetic lottery or swimming, biking or running at an elite level since the age of six, I want to show that pretty much anyone who is willing and able to do the work can tread water at the start line with the best athletes in the world at the Ironman World Championships in Hawaii.

CHAPTER 2

Tom

We were packed up and ready to leave, our bikes were disassembled and safely packed in their travel cases, the cycling kit was put away and all three of the bike boxes and our luggage were wedged into our small rental car. The day stretched out luxuriously ahead of us and I sat in the car enjoying the gorgeous summer sunshine and crisp, clean alpine air blowing in through the open window.

Our flight wasn't departing until that evening, which meant we had the whole day to enjoy the French summer sunshine. I also intended to indulge in some good French coffee and freshly-baked cake in the café in the tiny alpine village.

We pulled into the car park and Tom turned to me and suggested that we ride up one more time. He was talking about riding up Alpe d'Huez, one of the most iconic and famous Tour de France mountain climbs. I groaned and told him that there was no way I was riding up again. I added that, if we did, I would be the one rebuilding the three bikes I had spent hours disassembling and packing that morning. I would also have to break them down after riding up the mountain and repack them again.

'No way, Tom,' I said. 'You might never get back here again,' he warned. 'You don't know where you'll be in a year, or what will be happening in your life. You could be dead. And isn't that the only reason you flew all the way across Europe? To ride up this mountain?' I couldn't argue with any of his points. I had flown all the way across Europe to ride this mountain and I guess I didn't really know where I'd be in a year either.

We were in a small village called Bourg d'Oisans at the foot of Alpe d'Huez, which we had already ridden three times that week while we were over to watch a couple of stages of the Tour. I grudgingly admitted to myself that Tom was right, it was the reason we were in that place and there was no reason not to ride it again. After all, we weren't rushing to catch a flight. Maybe this would be my last chance to ride the climb. I still cursed him and grumbled as I started pulling the bike boxes out of the car.

Three months later, I was in work and got a call from Tom. 'I have some bad news,' he said. 'I have cancer.' I was shocked. Tom was maybe ten or fifteen years older than me, but he was still only in his early fifties. He was also the fittest person I knew; he had outpaced me on Alpe d'Huez every time we rode it. In typical 'Tom' fashion he fought his condition tooth and nail and six months later I got a call from him to say that he had been given the all-clear. The operation had been successful, as had the chemotherapy, and the doctors were confident that they had treated all the cancer.

During the same conversation, he asked if we were planning on going back to the Alps the following summer to watch the Tour and ride the mountains again. He said he would be there if we were. Of course, I said that we would make another trip so we booked our flights and accommodation, and planned which mountains to ride and which stages of the Tour de France to watch.

It wasn't long before Tom was texting me to say he was back out on the bike and that he too had booked his flights for July. However, at the end of May, I got another call from him to say that the cancer was back and that this time it was worse and the doctors had only given him weeks to live.

When I visited him for the last time in the hospice he was gaunt and frail. All of the lean muscle was gone and his skin seemed to hang directly off his bones. He was barely a shadow of the force he had been riding up Alpe d'Huez only ten months earlier. He asked me about our plans for July and wanted to know about the climbs we would ride and how training was going. Before I left he told me that I was to ride the Alpe d'Huez for him. He died shortly before we flew out.

As we pulled into Bourg d'Oisans again that July, all I could think about was what he had said to me a year before: 'You might never get back here again. You don't know where you will be in a year, or what will be happening in your life. You could be dead...' It has turned out to be one of the most influential things anyone has ever said to me. For the first time, I realised just how short and tenuous our grip on life is and that it can be taken from us at any stage without warning.

Ever since then, I've had an urgency and impatience to get things done. Things that felt important couldn't wait because I didn't know how much time I would have to do them. That doesn't mean that I only allow limited time to do something before giving up, rather that if I really want something then I want to start working for it now; there simply isn't time to wait.

Tom taught me that those who wait to be ready will lose out to those who are willing to just start and figure things out as they go. He also taught me that the outcome sometimes matters less than the fact that I was willing to start and to keep on trying.

The sense of satisfaction of emptying the tank, of giving something all that you have, of racing to the absolute best of your ability, regardless of the result, can far outweigh an easily-achieved victory.

CHAPTER 3

Starters get things done

I learnt early on in my life that there are two types of people: those who do things (starters) and those who plan on doing things (planners). Those who plan on doing things wait until everything is ready and perfect before starting; those who do things start as soon as possible, almost always before everything is ready and then fix the problems they encounter as they go.

I always believed that the starters were invariably the ones who succeed in getting things done. I saw again and again that the planners often never even started. Things were just never quite ready or the time was not right.

I don't know that it was ever a conscious decision to become someone who just started regardless of whether I had it all figured out or not, but after Tom died I decided that I wasn't going to waste a day of my life. The fifty or sixty years I had anticipated stretching out ahead of me might well turn out to be only twenty or fifteen, or less if what happened to Tom was anything to go by.

I'm a firm believer in just starting – you can correct the direction of a moving vehicle, but you can't correct anything if it's standing still. It might seem obvious, but taking that first step is the most important. When we decided to try to get me to Kona in 2011, we had no idea what was going to be involved. We didn't know if I had to train six times a week or fifteen. We didn't know if I needed to do six hours or thirty.

So I started training and, at the same time, I started researching how to do it. I started where we all do when we don't know something – on Google. Of course, about a trillion answers came up, all of them different: 'I got to Kona on an average of six hours a week', someone claimed. 'Fantastic,' I thought. 'I can do six hours of training a week.' It hadn't occurred to me that I was already doing about six hours a week and wasn't moving any closer to being a Kona competitor.

The next answer Google threw up said that Kona qualifiers typically do eighteen to twenty hours a week. 'Shit, that sounds like a lot,' I thought. Another claimed that Kona qualifiers can put in up to thirty hours a week. Thirty hours! Jesus, how the hell would I fit that in? How could I possibly go from my current six to ten hours that I had started doing four weeks previously, to thirty? That meant five hours a day, six days a week. Add in eight hours of sleeping and eight to ten hours of work and I was at twenty-four already. Where the hell was I going to fit in washing, shopping, getting to and from training, getting to work and cooking?

16

'Shit,' I thought. 'Maybe this isn't such a good idea after all.'

Wincing in anticipation of Aisling's response to the idea of training thirty hours a week, I just dropped it into conversation one day, quickly adding that another website reckoned I could do it on eighteen to twenty hours. I thought that if I presented the worst-case scenario first, then the second scenario would seem appealing in comparison. As usual, Aisling saw the problem in a different light and as a result saw a different solution.

We should get a coach to teach us what we need to know,' she answered, 'someone who actually knows what they're talking about, as opposed to someone who, for instance, had just read a load of random shit off the internet…' So we went and found a coach. And it became immediately apparent that, up to that point, I didn't have a clue about what I was doing. Either that, or he was trying to kill me.

In my first eight days with the new coach I did twenty-eight hours of training, including a race on the eighth day. It was a race that I rode almost 40 km to and home from, a race in which I won my age group and was placed third overall.

Both of these were things I'd never done before. It was like someone gave me the missing piece of the 'how to get fast' puzzle and it was the most obvious one imaginable. All I had to do was train lots. There wasn't any magic or any secret combination of intervals that I didn't know about. Neither was it about doing a certain drill or buying a special bike or set of nice carbon fibre wheels. It was simple: just do a shit-ton of training, way more than I would ever have thought prudent or even possible.

Even though I had been doing the wrong thing for a while, I had been doing something, and that something meant I could more-or-less handle the massive jump in training without completely breaking down (at least for a short period). The breaking down would come later, but we will come back to that in another chapter.

Now, it is important to note that I am not advocating a 300–500% increase in your training volume in one week, I am simply saying that if you have not tried the big volume approach and are stuck on a plateau, then it is the lowest of the low-hanging fruit. It is also the biggest piece of fruit on the tree. In fact, you could say it *is* the tree.

There are, however, a couple of things that you probably need to do differently if you are trying to introduce much bigger volume than you have tried before, which we will look at in the next chapter.

CHAPTER 4

How to do big volume

'I can only recall one athlete in my history of coaching [close to a decades-worth] who trained over 1,000 hours a year and didn't qualify [and he did qualify off that base the following year]. Given the time commitment and a bit of persistence, a Kona slot is a realistic possibility for just about everyone.' – Alan Couzens

Just do the work. The quality is often less important than the fact that you just get it done. Your body will tell you if you're going too hard – it usually won't let you train the next day or, if it does, the quality will be compromised. So listen to your body and do the work at a level that you can maintain consistently. If you do that, you will accumulate enough hours and you will become faster.

That was one of the biggest surprises for me: just how much it was possible to improve with a huge increase in training. I'm not sure where I thought the extra speed would come from before I made this 'discovery'; maybe some secret set of intervals or a magic combination of training sessions that the coach or someone else would let me in on? What I hadn't expected was that it would be as simple as 'train more'.

This is also the secret that most people don't want to know about. I was giving a talk to a group of triathletes recently and, after telling the story of how I learnt that training twenty to thirty hours a week made me fast, the first question I was asked was: 'If you don't want to train twenty hours a week, how else do you get faster?' It was like they hadn't been listening to me saying that there wasn't any secret sauce, no magic set of intervals, but just a lot of work. They didn't want to know that. They wanted the shortcut.

But for those willing to do the work and willing to stick with it for a long time, the most important part is as simple as: train lots, for a very long time. Of course, there was more to it than just training twenty hours a week. A couple of other things had to happen for this 'magic' to work and some of these happened by accident, while some happened by design. Surprisingly, most of them run counter to what you would expect.

If the first big secret was to do a shit-load of training, then the second was to slow down. This one didn't really happen by design as much as by circumstance. Aisling and I did a lot of our training together that first year and, in both swimming and running, it didn't really have much impact on how we trained.

We ran at a similar speed on most runs, except when we were doing faster intervals. So running together was fine. When you're swimming it's not like you can talk and train anyway and you're in a contained environment, so moving at different speeds wasn't an issue.

The bike, however, was a different matter. Aisling was fairly new to cycling and was a bit slower than me, but we enjoyed each other's company and we wanted, as much as was possible, to ride together. So I slowed down a little and this was one of the keys to being able to handle the massive jump in training hours.

I discovered that if I was riding slower than I normally did, then I could easily manage the extra hours. Another bonus was that time spent in the saddle at that easy effort was more effective at building my aerobic engine than all the time spent previously in what we now call the 'grey zone'. It turns out that training your aerobic engine, which is basically your fitness or how long you can ride for, happens most effectively at a fairly low easy effort or heart rate.

Ironically, the biggest difficulty with actually doing this is that it feels too easy and, because of this, a lot of recreational athletes train a little harder most of the time. Going above this heart rate moves you into a completely different training zone that has a very limited effect on aerobic fitness. A result of training in the incorrect zone is that fitness plateaus quickly. Athletes often either just accept that this is how fast they are capable of being or they try training harder and faster. Unfortunately, this has a limited benefit for endurance sports if it's not balanced with long and easy sessions.

That's not to say that training hard or doing intervals doesn't work. It does, but in order to see those benefits you need to move way above the middle zone in which most people spend most of their time. It's almost impossible to do this if you are tired from doing the rest of your training too hard. For the most part, easy should be easy, hard should be hard, and stay out of the middle.

So, if the first thing I did was increase the volume and the second thing was to slow down, then the third aspect of being able to train eighteen to twenty-five hours a week was to do most of it on the bike or in the water, where there was a lower risk of injury.

I think that the biggest effect that massive volume has on an athlete, if done correctly, is that it increases the size of their engine. I started out with the equivalent of a tiny, 600cc Smart car engine. By the time I reached Ironman UK five months later, I had something that was more akin to a three-litre V8. If I had started by introducing hard intervals first, instead of volume, I would have effectively been turbo charging a 600cc engine.

By working at a low enough intensity so that I could almost quadruple my training load, I was instead building a whole new engine – one that was bigger, more efficient, stronger and could race for almost as long as I wanted.

There is a time and place to be a super-charged Smart car, but Ironman is not it. As I got to know more of the guys who made it to Kona, the more I came to realise that, in many respects, I was no different to them: they train a lot and they have built their lives to allow for that. They consciously forgo other aspects of what might be considered a 'normal life' to live the life of an athlete.

CHAPTER 5

Training – how much is a lot?

There's a trend in the triathlon media towards articles that tell you how to get to Kona on ten hours of training a week. In my experience, that just doesn't happen for ninety percent of us. Of course, there are outliers and exceptions to this but, for the most part, an average of eighteen to twenty hours of training a week is the norm for Kona qualifiers.

There are also a growing number of athletes who are consistently hitting twenty-five to thirty hours a week. These athletes are effectively semi-professional, although they race as age groupers. This level of commitment obviously requires a very extreme lifestyle, but firstly, getting to Kona and secondly, being successful there, takes an extreme level of commitment.

Allowing that most Kona athletes will do at least one, and more often two, big days each week of between four to seven hours, that leaves four days to do the other seven-to-twelve hours of training. This is where the real numbers differ between Kona qualifiers and the rest of the field. Kona qualifiers average two to three hours a day, while regular athletes will usually do one big day at the weekend of four to six hours and around an hour a day for the rest of the week, to give them a total of between nine to eleven hours a week of training.

So is that all there is to it? Increase your volume from ten to twenty hours a week and you'll punch your ticket to the big island? Essentially yes, but it depends on a number of factors. In some ways it is that simple, but like a lot of simple ideas the reality of actually doing it is far from simple.

So how do you fit in twenty hours a week of training? For me, a typical training week might look something like this:

Monday 1st (1 session: 2 hr 30)
Run 2 hr 30, 30 km
Tuesday 2nd (2 sessions: 2 hr 35)
Swim 1 hr 30, 4000 m
Run 1 hr 05, 13 km
Wednesday 3rd (1 session: 1 hr)
Swim 1 hr, 3000 m
Thursday 4th (2 sessions: 3 hr 25)
Swim 1 hr 25, 4000 m
Run 2 hr, 24 km
Friday 5th (3 sessions: 4 hr 55)
Run 1 hr 05, 11 km easy
Bike 3 hr 15, 95 km
Run 35 min, 6 km easy

Saturday 6th (2 sessions: 1 hr 10)

Run 45 min, 7 km easy jog

Strength and conditioning (S&C) 25 min

Sunday 7th (2 sessions: 6 hr 30)

Bike 5 hr 30, 170 km

Run 1 hr, 11 km

Weekly Totals

Hours/Sessions

Total 22 hr 05: 13 sessions

Swim 3 hr 55, 11 km: 3 sessions

Bike 8 hr 45, 265 km: 2 sessions

Run 9 hr, 102 km: 7 sessions

S&C 25 min: 1 session

This is a week taken straight from my training diary and you can see that there are two big days in there: Friday and Sunday. Even with two short days (Wednesday and Saturday) at only around an hour each, the rest of the days are all between 2.5 and 3.5 hours. The key to this level of training is to have a very flexible lifestyle and supportive family and friends.

Without fail, every Kona qualifier that I've gotten to know ticks both of these boxes; it's very difficult to fit what is essentially another very hard, physical job into your life without these key aspects being in place. Alan Ryan, a six-time Kona qualifier with two Kona podiums to his name, is another very good example of how to get the work done. Alan has a slightly different approach to mine; he throws in lots of short sessions whenever the opportunity arises. He kept a blog of all of his training for the first half of 2016 and kindly allowed me to reproduce a week here for reference.

Week 9

Monday 22 February
2 hr 30 morning turbo steady/hard. 22C 2 x water bottles. Good honest effort.
1hr very tough club swim.
Total: 3 hr 30

Tuesday 23 February
1 hr 30 morning turbo. Hard, continuous effort. Good session. 1hr tough evening turbo. 24–25C 1st 20 min >330 watt (still dodgy reading), 5 min easy recovery pushed to finish but faded a bit. Average 280 Watt to finish. 260 Watt average overall – felt like an over 300 Watt session of a while ago but I faded a good bit towards the end. In my defence, I had to deal with crying/fighting kids a few times while fighting for breath, which didn't help concentration or rhythm. Good, hard effort though.
Total: 2 hr 30

Wednesday 24 February
45 min morning turbo. Higher cadence c.90 rpm. Easy effort. Legs a bit heavy from yesterday. A good easing out of the legs. Included some single leg drills and really concentrating on

pedalling technique. Trying to keep pressure off knees and using glutes and hips, spinning circles and keeping power even throughout.

1 hr 15 lunchtime swim. Jumped into another's session. Good warm-up. Main set included 16×100s coming in around 1:30. Nice swim. Felt I was going OK.

30 mins evening S&C.

Total: 2 hr 30

Thursday 25 February

1 hr early morning turbo. 21C. Started slow and steadily picked up pace. Cadence average 80, 40 min c.270 Watt. Good solid session, felt OK. Bit fecked towards end but held the watts.

2 hr lunchtime turbo. 22C two water bottles. Had intended to include an interval session but got into a good rhythm and tempo during the short warm-up and felt like continuing on. Good (relative) power numbers – probably akin to half IM race pace for 90 mins. Finished last 15 mins with cool down and single leg technique stuff.

Good tough effort. Ran out of water towards end and probably got a bit dehydrated. Was a bit 'shook' for rest of the day. Power Av. 270 though again felt a deal harder.

Total: 3 hr

Friday 26 February

Got set up for a morning cycle but got off after eight minutes. I am still trying to finish a painting for an exhibition coming up soon. I had been painting late into last night but had mucked it up a bit and it was annoying me. I couldn't settle and got off to make changes. Also it has to be said my arse was killing me and consequently I couldn't fire myself up for an hour or two in the saddle.

1 hr 30 evening swim. Steady 5km concentrating on technique. Pace felt very comfortable and my stroke seemed to hold together.

Total: 1 hr 30

Saturday 27 February

5 hr turbo. 20C rear killing me. Three hours down on my new Wheelworx Tri-Bars. One hour standing using big gear to alleviate the discomfort from the saddle. Av. Cadence 50. One hour back down on tri-bars. Overall a fairly easy if uncomfortable effort. Still good to have stuck it out if only to notch up a few hours in and out of the saddle.

Tried an evening run but stopped after 2 mins. Ankle not right at all.

Total: 5 hr

Sunday 28 February

1 hr morning turbo. Numb. Reasonable session. Long hard intervals with short recovery. Not maximum all-out efforts. 6-8 min efforts at 300 of my watts. (kept going a bit longer if the music was good). Intended a longer session but rear too sore to do more than the hour.

An afternoon spent snoring through an Alvin and the Chipmunks road trip to the cinema for recovery.

Total: 1 hr

Weekly Total: 19 hours

Swim 3 hr 45

Bike 14 hr 45
Run 0
S&C 30 min

Turbo training

The first thing that jumps out is that Alan does almost all of his biking on the turbo. This reflects in his biking in two ways: he is consistently one of the strongest bikers in his age group, but he is quick to point out that his bike handling does tend to suffer a little due to the lack of riding outdoors.

Having a turbo trainer for most of us is probably the most important piece of training equipment we possess, not only in terms of training benefit but also convenience and the fact that it allows us to ride regardless of the weather or climate. If you also have the luxury of being able to leave it set up permanently with a bike on it and ready to go, it means that if you only have an hour to fit in a session, fifteen or twenty minutes of that available hour aren't spent finding the kit, setting it up and putting it away afterwards.

I'm a big believer that removing obstacles to starting a training session means that you are more likely to do it. If all I have to do is throw on shorts and shoes and start, then I am much more likely to do it than if I have to go and try to remember where the hell I left my turbo skewer or front wheel riser block. If these small annoyances waste ten to fifteen minutes, then a tired, stressed athlete is just as likely to throw in the towel and skip the session.

Short sessions

The second thing I noticed when I first started following Alan's blog was the number of short sessions he did. Some days he would do three turbo trainer rides of between sixty to ninety minutes each, but would end up with a decent three to five hour day as a result. I'd never really considered doing three sessions a day on the turbo to get the time done. If I wanted to get a four-hour ride in I'd either get up earlier or move it to a day where I had more time available in one block. Alan, on the other hand, throws in a session whenever the opportunity presents itself and he doesn't worry whether it's thirty minutes or two hours.

Commuting

Another friend of mine who is quite time-constrained, particularly at work, includes all of his commuting in his training. He manages to include eight-to-twelve hours a week of his training in his daily commute to and from work. He is also very careful not to just cycle or run in; every commute has a purpose. Even if that purpose is just a recovery ride, it's mapped out. He doesn't just get sucked into the usual commuter races.

A typical week for him would look like this:

Monday
AM: Bike commute 60 min, including 5 x 6 min big gear work
Lunch: Swim 45 min
PM: Bike commute 60 min, including 45 min top of zone 2 heart rate (Z2)
Tuesday

AM: Bike commute 60 min, including 45 min Z2
PM: Bike commute 60 min, including 5 x 3 min hard, recover 1 min between

Wednesday

AM: Bike commute 60 min all easy
Lunch: Swim 45 min
PM: Run commute 90 min, including 60 min top of Z2

Thursday

AM: Run commute 60 min Z1-Z2
Lunch: Long swim 90 min
PM: Bike commute 60 min, including 45 min top of Z2

Friday
Off

Saturday

Bike 4 hr 30
Run 30 min off bike
Sunday
Run 2.5 hr

This athlete also hits over eighteen hours for an average week during an Ironman build period, and what's worth noting about him is that his commute in the car or by public transport takes between fifty and seventy minutes on average, so in reality his mid-week training isn't taking any time out of his life. Two of the swims he fits into his normal lunch break, then eats at his desk in the afternoon. His work days are fairly long and he almost never leaves on time, so taking one long lunch break is something he's negotiated with his employer as a result.

Most of the year his training doesn't impact his family life at all. His wife works Saturday so that is always his long training day and he's usually finished his long run by 10 am on Sunday, just in time to cook breakfast.

During the heaviest training period leading into his Ironman, he takes one half day from work during the week for four weeks, and one full extra day off for the following four weeks, and does two big training days each week.

One of the things he pointed out to me is that his half-day from work is always in the morning, not the afternoon. When he initially tried taking the afternoon off, he found himself often not getting out of the office on time and losing half of his planned training time as a result. He found that this never happened when he was only starting work at 1pm Having a deadline meant that he knew he needed to get up early and start training so as to be finished by the time he needed to go to work.

Training Camps

Training camps are one of the best ways to bump up your training hours but there are some important things to consider when planning one. We typically do training camps in the winter to load up on cycling, and for most people this is the safest way to massively overload while minimising the risk of injury.

1,000 km weeks on the bike aren't unheard of for the top age groupers on a training camp, but if your normal weekly distance is in the range of 300–400 km, then a 50% increase is probably more in line with what you should be aiming for. If you couple this with adding 50% to your normal swim distance, your hours for the week will be significant, even before you factor in running.

Mini camps

I've tried big camps of up to two weeks and mini training camps of four days. While both work, the most surprising thing was the effect that the four-day camps had on my fitness, while also having less impact on the rest of my life. Disappearing for four days has much less impact on work and puts less pressure on home life than being gone for a week or longer.

Mini camps also have a couple of extra benefits:

1. They are more repeatable. I can easily fit two training camps of four days into an eight-week period without frying myself or coming home to find a suitcase on the doorstep. My recovery after a four day cycling-based camp is fast; I often only need one day off and a light day afterwards before a return to normal training.

2. Because they are shorter, there is less temptation to put a session off like there might be in a longer camp, so they are very compressed and efficient. I'm always careful not to waste time on such a short camp.

Example of a mini training camp:

Thursday

Bike 5 hr 55, 160 km
Swim 35 min, 2,100 m easy

Friday

Swim 50 min, 3000 m
Bike 6 hr 30, 162 km 1900m ascent
Run 30 min, 6 km off bike

Saturday

Bike 6 hr 35, 170 km
Sunday
Bike 6 hr 30, 171.5 km

This is a four-day mini camp I built around a cycle sportif event that we sponsor. Part of our sponsorship for the event is that we provide mechanical support through our bike shop. I used to send a mechanic in our van to look after any technical problems that came up, but it occurred to me that I could combine work and training by doing both the mechanical support and riding my bike. One of the event staff drives the van with the tools, spares and workshop set-up and if there's an issue I stop with the rider and fix the bike.

Quite often the pace of these rides is considerably easier than my regular rides so I add in extra training load by doing most of the day in the biggest gear I can push. If the day is shorter than I had planned, I would add in extra training afterwards. Riding 150–180 km in the biggest gear on your bike has a massive training effect, even if you're riding at a slower pace with much slower riders.

The other type of training stress I add on these events is that, after fixing a mechanical issue, I chase back to the group. I do this flat out, like I would ride threshold intervals. I might do this once, twice or a half-dozen times in a day, depending on the number of mechanical problems.

I never bothered riding these events before, thinking that because it was too slow compared to my normal pace it wouldn't be of much benefit. However, because it's very aerobic I'm able to do a massive overload and recover much faster than I would from a faster, harder camp.

Summary

1. Lots of short sessions can add up to a lot of training if that's the only way you can fit it in. Just because we are

training for a long race and we are aiming to do big volume, not all sessions need to be long, epic ones. If the only way to get a lot of the work in is to do it in lots of small bite-sized pieces, then that works too.

2. The turbo is your friend, or at least it should be. If possible, make it a permanent fixture in your spare room, if you have one. Having your 'home gym' set up so that you can quickly and easily take advantage of a free hour means there's no time lost setting up the turbo.

3. Managing your work hours to fit in your training may involve starting a little late, taking a long lunch or finishing a little early. These are all ways that you can fit in the extra sessions required.

4. If your work hours aren't flexible enough to allow you to fit in the extra training required, then maybe look at your commute. Can you commute some or all of your journey on your bike or on your feet? If so, you can minimise the impact training has on both your work and family life.

CHAPTER 6

How many hours do you train?

We are all interested and curious about just how much training the other guys do. Maybe we are even a little obsessed. In a sport where many people believe that more training trumps all else, 'How many hours do you train?' is a question that is asked again and again.

In writing this book I asked a number of Kona qualifiers and professional athletes for their help. I asked them the questions that I wanted answered: How many hours did they train? What did they think was the most important recipe for success in getting to Kona? What was their lifestyle like and how did they fit everything in? I asked these questions in part to learn how others do it and if what they did applied to me, and partly just out of plain old curiosity.

What the age groupers say about training hours

Andy Kinnane

'The amount of training hours depends on the time of year, but when in full training and not peak time I'd say twelve to fifteen hours average. This might nudge up to twenty hours at peak. I generally fit in three sessions in each discipline, but also have two to three strength and conditioning sessions per week to help make it all possible. Good S&C work is free speed in my opinion, so it's not all about rehab.'

Emmet Kelly

'As with all training plans your time increases the closer you get to your main event. At the height of training, I'd be at twenty-two hours. Four swims of one-hour sessions, four to five bikes for a total of about ten hours, four runs about six hours. I'd also do a Pilates class and a gym session and include stretching every morning. Aside from the peak weeks, I would stay over sixteen hours a week for months.'

It's remarkable how similar the overall hours these athletes train for are and the breakdown between the three sports. Or maybe it isn't that remarkable after all. Maybe it's just a matter of accumulating enough training hours over a long enough period of time?

Kevin Gilleece

Kevin's hours are almost a carbon copy of Emmet's: 'I train every day when following a plan. Probably hit a maximum of twenty hours split nine hours on the bike, six-and-a-half of running and four-and-a-half of swimming.'

John Newsom

John Newsom is one of the best-known voices in our sport and has raced as a professional and now as an age grouper. John shared a typical week's training during an Ironman build, typically it's twelve to fifteen hours, depending on the length of the long ride:

> Mon: run with intervals + core 90 min
> Tue: AM swim 3 km, PM Bike 1.5 hrs
> Wed: long run
> Thur: bike/run 2 hr
> Fri: swim 3 km
> Sat: run/bike 1 hr
> Sun: long ride

Bevan James Eyles

Bevan James Eyles is John Newsom's sidekick on their IMTalk podcast, or maybe Bevan would tell you John is his sidekick. Either way, Bevan is a very accomplished athlete, as well having qualified for Kona.

During an Ironman build, training is between fifteen to twenty hours for Bevan. He will average three to four swims, four bikes and two to three runs. The difference for him though is that because he works in the fitness industry he also teaches and takes part in a dozen fitness classes a week.

Garron Mosley

'During an Ironman block I will train between fourteen and seventeen hours a week. Three hours swimming, six to seven hours of running and the rest will be made up on the bike.'

What the professionals say about training hours

Emma Bilham

'Anything between eighteen and thirty hours, but usually around twenty-two to twenty-five. It's broken down as five to six swims a week and alternating bike and run days. For example: first day swim and double bike or long bike, next day swim and double run.'

Jocelyn Gardner McCauley

'[As an age grouper] I qualified for Kona on an average of fourteen fourteen-hour weeks. The maximum was an eighteen-hour week (but that was only one week).'

'As a professional I train between twenty to thirty hours a week, depending on whether they're light or heavy. I honestly don't track it at all. The split is about ten to fifteen hours of biking, three to seven hours running and four to seven hours of swimming.'

On fitting training in as an age grouper before turning professional

Lots of age group athletes think that if we didn't have to work, we could train as much as the professionals and could race alongside them. Jocelyn's answer about how she fitted in training as a top-level age grouper highlighted that being a professional athlete is more than just having all day to train.

Jocelyn Gardner McCauley

When she was working a high pressure and demanding job as a nurse, which involved switching between day and night shifts, she did things that would be considered crazy by most athletes, never mind the general public. I worked nights years ago and the only thing I was able for after a night shift was sleep. I couldn't get my head around heading out for a hard five-hour group ride after being awake at work all night.

'As a nurse I had to start training very early (4 am) on days that I worked. I worked three twelve-hour days so I would train more on days I didn't work. I still had my daughter, so I did most of my training inside on the trainer and treadmill. I did my long rides on Sunday and I remember working night shifts on Friday night till 7:30 am and meeting people straight from work for a five-hour ride. There was a lot of that'

CHAPTER 7

Maintaining your lifestyle

Consistency is probably the most important factor and one that is so often overlooked. If you've got an ambition to get to Kona and if, like me, it's going to take you eighteen months or longer to get fit and strong enough to achieve that goal, then where you pull that extra training time from has to be sustainable. If you're at six hours of training a week now, work sixty-plus hours and have young children, then you've got two areas of your life already competing heavily for your time.

The first choice you'll have to make is where the extra eight to twelve hours a week come from: work or family? If you think it's going to be from family time, then you need to be certain that you have the support from them. It's also very important that they understand what's actually involved. They might think that the idea and the challenge are exciting initially, but if they don't know what's required for the next year-and-a-half, then discovering you missing for another six-hour training day or, worse yet, asleep on the couch after a six-hour training day, unable to participate in normal family life, it can become very old, very quickly. If the time is going to come from work, can you afford to drop those hours?

For a number of Kona qualifiers I know who have families, the hours spent training mostly come from work. This can have an impact on lifestyle, spending power and more. These athletes usually make a conscious decision to forgo or limit career and monetary pursuits in favour of a life focused around training and racing. This isn't necessarily seen as a sacrifice, rather it's just a choice they make about how to live their lives. It's more important to them to live the life they desire, than to have a more financially successful or career-focused lifestyle. It also isn't always permanent, they might decide that for a certain period a lifestyle as an athlete is worth foregoing career advancement or taking a hit in earnings.

At the moment we run two businesses, but are fortunate enough to be able to mostly choose the hours we work for the best part of the year. The bike shop is busiest during the spring and summer, at weekends and in the evenings. As a result, I work pretty much every Saturday and Sunday but then take Monday and Tuesday (the quietest days) off as my 'weekend'.

Wednesday, Thursday and Friday the store opens until 9pm and the afternoons and evenings are the busiest times, so I typically don't start work until 2pm and stay on until 9pm. This allows me to train pretty much every day before work. On the weekends, for most of the year, I also don't have to start until

12 or 1pm, so I can also fit in a decent training session before both of those work shifts.

While training fifteen to twenty hours a week has to take time from our normal life, I try to limit its impact. The choice was, where possible, to take the majority of the time from the business. I think this is the best solution for us, because it means that Ironman training and racing isn't causing stress at home by taking over everyone's life. It has also forced me to become very efficient while I am in work. Fewer hours spent in the business mean I can't waste time when I'm there, so I've learnt to do the same volume of work in less time.

A friend of mine bargained with his company to let him work a half day every Friday for his twelve biggest training weeks, allowing him to do three big days at the weekend without compromising too much of his time with his family. Friday's long day came from work time. Saturday was his normal long day, but he started at 6 am and was done by lunchtime. Sunday was his long run and, again, he started early and was done before most people's days had even started. When he was finished he could do the kids football stuff and drive dad's taxi for the afternoon.

However you do it, if Kona is your ultimate goal you need to find an extra twenty-five hours a week most weeks. I hear you shout 'twenty-five? You said eighteen to twenty!' Yes, you're right, I did, but one of the things that the triathlon magazines don't tell you about getting to Kona by training just ten hours a week, is that you also need to allow an extra five or more hours out of your life for preparation, washing and travelling to and from training.

Unless you have a swimming pool in your spare room, you need to allow time to and from your pool at least three times a week, and don't forget to add in the fifteen minutes before and after each swim you need to get changed and showered. You will also likely become very well-acquainted with laundry, shopping for food and food preparation. You will wash and dry more kit than you can imagine and you will go from training to eating to sleeping to training to eating to work to eating, and all that food needs to be prepared, because you won't get to Kona eating Big Macs.

To fit everything in, we plan out each week in advance. Aisling and I have our iPhone calendars synced and we schedule everything: training, work, appointments, even time off from both work and training. That way there aren't any unexpected surprises. Having allocated time to do my sessions means I tend to start on time, because I almost always have something else booked for immediately afterwards.

A typical day's calendar might look like this:

> Tuesday
> Off work, off training

Or this:

> Wednesday
> 07:30–09:30 Swim, 1 hr 20
> 10:00–11:15 Walk the dogs
> 11:30–13:30 Bike, 2-hr turbo
> 13:30–14:00 Food, shower and head into work
> 14:00–21:00 Work

The entire week can be laid out like this and it means that we both know exactly when we have time to train, work or take a day off completely. We've found that this level of planning and communication helps eliminate stress at home; it also makes us realise just how much time we spend each day getting to and from the pool, getting ready for training or doing any of the other jobs that need to be done to allow training. Things like visiting the bike shop, laundry, shopping for food or cooking meals. All of these things need to be considered and planned for as part of an athlete's lifestyle.

A broken bike or broken turbo trainer isn't just an inconvenience, it's a missed training session, or two, or four, and inconsistency is one of the things that will put an end to any hopes of a fast Ironman or Kona slot quicker than almost anything else. You need to be extremely efficient with your training. If eighteen hours of training takes twenty-five hours out of your life, then it's going to take a lot of planning and discipline to keep that going for the twelve to twenty-four months needed for most of us to get to Kona.

Sleeping, drinking and eating

I don't know any Kona people or serious athletes who are also party animals. Well, not regular party animals anyway. They can sometimes last until midnight at the post-race party; sometimes, but not usually. Most of the really good ones don't drink alcohol, eat well and get plenty of sleep. These are just a couple more boxes that need to be ticked. If you want to be an athlete, you need to act like an athlete.

Summary

1. Decide where the extra training hours required will come from, then make sure that it is sustainable.

2. Get your family or significant other on board, structure work to fit in with the training, or both.

3. Eighteen hours of training is likely to take up to twenty-five hours out of your life. Schedule your training and everything you can to ensure you can fit it in.

4. Schedule time for food shopping, preparation and laundry. You will consume lots of one and produce lots of the other.

5. Schedule time off. If you are training close to twenty hours a week then your recovery is as important as the training.

CHAPTER 8

The big secret

I read a book called *Once a Runner* written by a guy called John L. Parker Jr. In fact it's one of the few books I've read more than once. It tells the story of a collegiate runner, a miler, who aspires to race at the Olympics. There's another runner featured in the story, a guy called Bruce Denton who has already been to the Olympics and has won a medal. Of course, everyone wants to run and train with this exotic creature and to learn the secret that turned him into an Olympic medallist.

When new athletes arrive at the college and show up for their first run with Denton they are amazed to find that the pace of the ten-mile morning run is not only manageable but almost easy compared to their usual training or race pace. That afternoon, they head out for their second run with Bruce, a track or interval session of some sort. They also handle that one comfortably and their confidence grows. But they are thinking that Denton is holding out on them. Maybe they haven't earned the right yet to be let in on 'the secret'.

Day two rolls around and they cruise through another comfortable morning ten-miler and, later that day, another afternoon run. On day three, they are starting to get a little tired and just a little sore, but they show for the early morning run and again knock out the nice, steady ten-miler. This time, however, it doesn't feel so easy.

By the time they've completed a week, or ten days, of two runs a day, with each week consisting of somewhere in the region of 130 miles, they realise they've discovered Denton's 'secret'. They also realise that they don't really like it. They see that there is no magic; there's just relentlessly crushing, consistent hard work, twice a day, every day, regardless of how tired they are or what the weather is like.

The gloss starts to fade from their dream and they first miss one session, then a day, then another, and then a few together as they decide that there has to be more to life than this. There has to be more to life than running and living like a monk. One-by-one, they all drop away and, once again, Denton is the only one left.

I have always thought that this perfectly sums up what is required to excel at any sport – at any pursuit in fact. Showing up, day after day, and doing the work almost automatically, without questioning, doubting or wavering from the single-minded pursuit of the one goal of excellence. I think it is also, by far, the hardest aspect of Ironman training. My first experience of just how difficult it was came just weeks into my first attempt at qualifying for Kona back in 2011.

The following is taken from my April 2011 training diary, just after I started with my first coach in my first year of trying to qualify for Kona:

> I started training with the coach on Saturday. We went to a training camp he had organised for the weekend. The first day started out with an eighty-minute swim in the endless pool, working on technique and getting video analysis done. After breakfast, we headed out on the bikes for a 90 km rolling, hilly ride. There was another swim session in the afternoon and then, before dinner, we did a ninety-minute run. This is the first time I've ever done four sessions in a day. I finished tired, but really enjoyed the day.
>
> Saturday 2nd
> Total: 6 hr 30
> Swim 1 hr 20, 2,000 m
> Bike 3 hr 40, 89 km
> Swim 40 min, 1,000 m
> Run 50 min, 9 km hill repeats
>
> Sunday 3rd
>
> Today was similar to yesterday, the only real difference being that there was only one swim session. I felt pretty good on the bike, but was definitely feeling the cumulative

effect of more than twelve hours of training in two days by
the end of the run.
Total: 5 hr 50
Bike 3 hr 30, 86 km
Swim 50 min, 1,000 m
Run 1 hr 30, 15 km

Monday 4th

Back to normal life today and this is the first real week of
following the coach's plan. 'Only' two sessions to do today
– a two-hour bike and a 4,000 metre swim. I'm feeling
good, strong and really enjoying the training so far. That
being said, I've really only done three days of it. It will be
interesting to see how I feel in a week, or four...
Total: 3 hr 25
Bike 2 hr, 72 km
Swim 1 hr 25, 4,000 m

Tuesday 5th

Day 5 and it's another two-session day, starting with a 19
km run and the second session was an hour in the pool.
Total: 2 hr 40
Run 1 hr 40, 19 km
Swim 1 hr, 2,500 m

Wednesday 6th

This is the first single session day so far and it almost feels
like a day off. Just eighty minutes on the bike.
Total: 1 hr 20
Bike 1 hr 20, 44 km

Thursday 7th

This was a decent day, almost five-and-a-half hours training. Felt good, if a little tired at the end.
Total: 5 hr 20
Bike 4 hr 30, 115 km
Run 50 min, 10.5 km

Friday 8th

'Just' a ninety-minute run today. Given that I've a race tomorrow, I reckon that I'll carry a lot of fatigue in after the biggest week's training I've ever done.
Run 1 hr 30, 16.5 km

Saturday 9th

We rode ninety minutes easy to and back from the race, which was a sprint triathlon today. I also had my best result to date. I placed third overall and I won my age group.
Total: 4 hr
Bike 1 hr 30, 34 km
Swim 20 min, 1,000 m
Bike 30 min, 20 km
Run 20 min, 5 km
Bike 1 hr 20, 38 km

This was an incredible feeling after just eight days of the new training. It's probably also worth noting that by close of business today, I'll have clocked up in excess of thirty hours training in the last eight days. To put that in context,

I did twenty hours total in January, thirty-three hours total in February and in March I managed a whopping fifty hours.

Then something happened…this is an excerpt from my training diary six weeks later, in May 2011.

Monday 9th
I'm too tired to train today. I've sessions in the plan but I just can't face it.

Tuesday 10th

I was really struggling in the pool and the run early today. I did an extra swim to make up for yesterday, despite being told not to. Coach was right and I got out of the pool after thirty minutes. I'm completely fucked.
Swim 1 hr, 3,200 m
Run 45 min, 10.5 km
Swim 30 min, 1,400 m

Wednesday 11th

Cut the swim short. Too tired to finish.
Bike 1 hr 50, 57 km
Swim 40 min, 2,000 m

Thursday 12th

Exhausted again today. Managed a 2,000 m swim but couldn't do the rest of the plan.
Swim 45 min, 2,000 m

Friday 13th

The tiredness is getting worse. I'm so tired all the time. I can't function in work and I'm not sleeping well. Fucking sick of this shit.
Swim 30 min, 1,400 m

Saturday 14th
Off

Sunday 15th
I managed an easy run today, but felt worse afterwards. Skipped the second session.
Run 1 hr, 12 km

Weekly Total: 7 hr 15 (8 sessions)
Swim 3 hr 25, 10,000 m
Bike 1 hr 50, 57 km
Run 2 hr, 22.5 km
Seven hours total training for the week and I'm still not recovered. I'm so tired all the time and still not sleeping. If I do fall asleep, I wake a while later soaked in sweat. I had to change pillows in the middle of the night. The lack of sleep is making it worse.

Monday 16th

Went out to do the ride that was on the plan and turned around after twenty minutes. I could hardly turn the pedals.
Bike 45 min, 23 km

Tuesday 17th
Off

Wednesday 18th
Off

Thursday 19th
Easy run. Still tired, but finally slept last night.
Run 50 min, 10 km

Friday 20th
I slept again last night. I'm finally starting to feel a little better.
Swim 45 min, 2,200 m

Saturday 21st
Bike 35 min, 16.5 km
Run 50 min, 9 km

Sunday 22nd
Finally started to feel good today and that's the first good session in weeks. Hoping I'm back on track.
Bike 5 hr 10, 151 km

Weekly total: 8hr 55 (6 sessions)
Swim 45 min, 2,200 m

Bike 6 hr 30, 190.5 km
Run 1 hr 40, 19 km

Doing the volume is one thing but being able to do it week in, week out and not burn out, get injured or quit when you realise just how long it takes and how grindingly hard it is, that's another thing entirely.

Things can seem easy at the start as you can see from my notes. There's the excitement of a new project and the novelty of all that training. It became increasingly difficult as fatigue and the brutal relentlessness of what was actually required sank in. It eventually got to the stage where I couldn't train at all and I lost weeks at a time. During my first eighteen months of trying to train like a Kona athlete, I regularly tipped myself over the edge through over-enthusiasm, stupidity or naïvety. I also think I did a lot of the training too hard in the beginning. This meant that I just couldn't manage the required volume; I was flattened as the intensity was too high. I take responsibility for these screw-ups, there's no blame being assigned to anyone other than myself.

The coach said that I wasn't Kona material when we originally approached him and, in a way, he was right. I'd never shown any potential to indicate that I was. What he didn't know was how dogged and determined I was, not to mention that I was afraid of failure and of being proven wrong. In a lot of ways, the only thing that got me to Kona was this aspect of my personality. My Dad calls it having a fire in your belly. Another word you may use to describe it is obsession.

Consistency, I think, is the single hardest part of the training – the idea of having to train for three hours a day, six days a week and having to do at least three swims, three bikes and three runs every single week, is so much harder than I could ever have imagined. Knowing when to push through or when to back off is also vital. Should you keep going if you're fatigued, or is rest more important? Being able to continue to train even when you're unmotivated, or the weather is bad, or when it looks like you'll never reach your goal, is what differentiates all the really good athletes we've worked with. It all comes down to consistency, which is one of the factors that I've always struggled with.

CHAPTER 9

Consistency

For anyone I've spoken to who is chasing a Kona slot, the average number of training hours per week ranges from sixteen to twenty-five. The level of commitment needed to hit that number of training hours week after week, with a full-time job and family, is extraordinary. Being consistent is mentioned and thrown around in training articles, but the reality of that one small word is that it is probably the most difficult part of really successful Ironman training.

I've always thought that consistency was one of the major contributors to my improvement as an athlete and all of the athletes I've spoken to mention it as well.

Owen Martin

Owen thinks that consistency is crucial, although he points out that it's only one of the many requirements for success: 'I think being uber consistent in your training is one of many things required to have a shot at Kona.'

Bryan McCrystal

Bryan, a current Irish Ironman record holder, also thinks consistency is a key component but that not overdoing it and recovery are often overlooked aspects of improvement: 'If I were to advise anyone, I'd say be consistent and realistic in what you can do. Being an amateur, the tendency is to push too hard and neglect recovery. Sometimes it's better to recover than train.'

Kevin Gilleece

Kevin, a two-time Kona qualifier, mentions consistency several times while being interviewed. He seems to rate it more highly than almost anything else in getting to Kona successfully: 'Willingness to hurt over and over again in training and learning to accept it.'

When I asked him about his craziest training session, he stressed the benefits of being a consistent trainer over doing the epic sessions that some athletes favour: 'There's no point doing a monster session and then having to take an extra day off because of it. Consistency trumps monster sessions. Being able to train day in, day out, in my opinion, is better than a huge session one day that leaves you flattened for three days.'

Emmet Kelly

Emmet gave a simple and straight to the point answer to what the most important factor in getting to Kona is: 'Consistency in training.'

While interviewing Emmet and looking into his background, I could see that consistency was a part of his life from when he was a kid. Years of commuting on his feet laid the groundwork for Emmet's killer run: 'I ran up and down to school and home for lunch. Just over 3 km each way, every day during secondary school.'

Bevan James Eyles

Looking at an athlete's history can sometimes give an insight into their current success. Bevan works in the fitness industry and, in his day job, teaches a dozen classes a week. He does this week in and week out and has done for years. Although it may not be Ironman-specific training, it has given him a massive base of strength and fitness upon which to then build an Ironman training programme and, as a result, he had a very successful Ironman career.

Andy Kinnane

Andy talks about the difficulties of being consistent in training and how much your life needs to be structured, planned and disciplined: 'It sounds boring, but consistency trumps everything. This is not as simple as it seems though. You need to be good at planning and time management. Being self-aware and knowing when to push and when not to. I would add a caveat to that too – consistency over a sustained period. This isn't a twelve month project!'

Emma Bilham

When asked what the single most important thing needed for success in middle and long distance racing was, Emma answered succinctly and to the point: 'Consistent training.'

CHAPTER 10

Breaking down, over-reaching and over-training

Most of what I've learnt has been from the coaches I've worked with, or in a good old-fashioned way: through making mistakes. One of the most important lessons I've learnt over the course of ten years racing Ironman, has been to make as many of those mistakes as possible in training, rather than in racing.

The mistake I made most often in the first couple of years was going too hard in training and frying myself. The best example of not only going too hard, but thinking I knew better than the coach was in the first year I was chasing Kona. I'd raced Ironman UK in August and about four weeks later I was back into regular training. The plan had me down to do a five-hour ride with a 10 km run off it. The exact session was to ride three times for one hour at Ironman race pace, with fifteen minutes of easy riding in between each hour-long interval. Then I was to run off the bike, starting very easy for the first thirty minutes, with the rest of the hour to be spent at my Ironman race pace.

What I actually did was a little bit different. I headed out on the bike and started the first interval after about fifteen minutes, as instructed. I settled into a comfortable effort, one I knew I could sustain for five hours, if needed. As I neared the end of the first hour, I was feeling really strong and seeing an average speed of close to 35 kph. I got excited at the prospect of doing the fastest ride I'd ever done in training, so I decided to stay on the gas and not take the fifteen-minute recovery.

I was a little intoxicated with the speed and just wanted to hang on to that average for a while longer. I was curious just how high I could get it and how long I could hang on to it for (there's some saying involving curiosity and a dead four-legged furry pet that may be relevant here).

I ate and drank as I was supposed to and reached the end of the second hour with the average speed still creeping up. Feeling strong and becoming more and more excited by the numbers, I kept on pushing through the third, fourth and fifth hours. In fact, I kept on going at that same pace all the way to 190 km. I was starting to hurt towards the end, but I was on such a high I did what was the fastest solo long bike ride I'd ever done either in or outside of racing, so I kept on pushing, despite the growing fatigue and discomfort.

I got off the bike with an average speed of 36 kph. This was by far the fastest I'd ever ridden for that distance. I felt like a superhero – completely fucking invincible.

I quickly changed shoes and headed out for the run. Still feeling like I was made of steel and could run through a brick wall, I once more disregarded the coach's advice for the rest of the session. Surely I knew my body better than him, and while I felt this good I was going to make the most of it.

I clocked off my first kilometre in just over four minutes. In my mind I started to write my acceptance speech as I took the Mdot trophy, for not only taking a Kona slot at my next race, but for also winning my age group at the upcoming Ironman in Florida.

Beep. The next kilometre went by faster, just under four minutes. 'Jesus, I'm flying', I thought to myself.

Beep, beep, beep. Three, four and five kilometres all went by as easily and as fast as the first two and in my mind I planned the next three days of massive training sessions. I had the weekend off work and Aisling was away so I thought I would do six hours a day, each day, and a couple of runs too. Then I thought I would get back to the coach's plan. He didn't need to know any of it – at least not until after I'd done it and could show him that I did actually know better than him. At which point, he would come to the staggeringly obvious conclusion that I was indeed a legend.

I cruised through the easiest forty-one minute 10 km of my life. I couldn't believe it. This training volume thing really works I thought, as I opened the fridge and proceeded to eat everything in sight. I texted the coach, giving him what I thought were the coolest training numbers I'd ever sent him, only to receive his reply. He wondered which part of the week's plan I'd seen that session on. He wasn't impressed. I thought I'd better not mention the fact that I was planning on extending the following day's two-hour ride by a further four. Or do six hours the day after that, instead of the one-hour swim he'd prescribed.

The next morning I couldn't get out of bed, I couldn't even wake up. After hitting the snooze button a half dozen times, I eventually dragged myself out of bed at 10 am. I ate breakfast and looked at the bike standing there, looking back at me all smug and fast-looking. I was so tired, even the thought of another long ride hurt.

'I'll feel better when I get going', I thought. Ninety minutes into the ride, with my average speed somewhere in the very low twenties, (that's still kilometres per hour, not miles) I pulled the plug, went home and got back into bed, telling myself I still had another two days to get the extra-long rides done.

Saturday and Sunday were worse. I was so tired that I didn't train either day and, just like that, I'd tipped myself over the edge. It took me another six weeks to recover, during which time every session I managed to do (and there were quite a few that I skipped) was a slog and I was exhausted all the time. By the time Ironman Florida came around, I was starting to feel better. However, any chance I had of taking a Kona slot or that place on the podium I had daydreamed about had been well and truly scuppered that day back in August.

What I had gone through, I think, was a moderate case of over-training. I say moderate because I recovered in less than two months. I've read cases where it takes athletes a year or more to recover from serious over-training. Over-reaching or breaking down is the point at which you reach your current limits and keep on pushing past them, but haven't gone as far as over-training.

I believe, and I'm open to correction by more knowledgeable folk, that over-reaching is more or less a normal part of pushing your limits. It can sometimes be an extreme way to progress and it is something that, if not managed correctly, can go quite badly, as you can see from my example above.

Warning signs of over-training

1. Not sleeping, poor/restless sleep or night sweats, despite high levels of fatigue.

2. Exhaustion is obviously one of the main signs, but it's not always clear if it's a normal level of fatigue or over-reaching.

3. I find that my mood is a very good indicator of fatigue levels, often better than just the fact that I'm tired. When I'm in heavy Ironman training it's normal to be tired almost all the time. Normal fatigue doesn't usually affect my mood though. If I start to get cranky, argumentative or my mood is bad, it's very often a sign that I'm heading into a state of over-reaching.

4. Sometimes these warnings are accompanied by feeling the opposite of what I might expect. In the instance above, physically I was in the best shape of my life and, despite that, I was sailing along the razor's edge, blissfully unaware that I was about to crash in the most catastrophic way. Aisling and the coach both warned me I was overdoing it, and both tried to rein me in. But, of course, I thought I knew better, so I ignored all the signs and their warnings and drove the bus straight over the edge of the cliff.

5. Another fairly reliable indicator is your resting heart rate. If your waking heart rate is significantly elevated from what it would normally be, then that is a good

indication that you're either reaching your limit, or about to tip over it.

6. Motivation is another indication for me that I'm reaching my limits. As I start to push past what I'm normally physically capable of, I often see a dip in motivation as I start to break down. I'm normally very highly motivated to train, so when I start not wanting to do the sessions, it's a warning that I'm getting close to my limit.

For a well-trained athlete, if it's caught in time, it often takes no more than a couple of easy training days or rest days to recover from over-reaching, before being able to resume normal sessions. Over-training on the other hand can take months to recover from, and may require an athlete to take a complete break from training.

I'm fairly old-school when it comes to training and technology and keep track of my daily sessions in an old-fashioned training diary, as opposed to using an app or computer programme. I also track four things other than my training:

1. Motivation

2. Energy

3. Sleep

4. Work

For motivation and energy, I just assign them a score out of ten, with one being no motivation and ten being highly motivated, and the same with energy levels. For sleep, I note the length of sleep in hours and if it was good or poor. For work, I note my hours and if it was a particularly difficult day.

The benefit of tracking these four metrics is that when I look back, they will usually reveal a pattern. For example, if both my work and training hours are consistently high for a period of time, then my fatigue level will start to rise and, at the same time, my motivation might start to drop.

Looking out for these trends is a good way to make training decisions, like whether to push through fatigue and keep training, or to back off. If your fatigue is 'normal' and the result of a big training load, rather than due to external (work or family stress) causes, then it may be a good idea to push through a previous barrier and possibly make a breakthrough. If, however, low motivation and fatigue is the result of an overload of work and training stresses, then backing off one or the other is probably the best option.

As long as I am tracking these four markers alongside my training hours and sessions, I can look back over a week or month and see a trend as my training load increases and fatigue builds. As a result, I can make a much more informed training or coaching decision.

You've probably guessed by now that I'm very low-tech and fairly old-school when it comes to training. I think there is more than one way to train, more than one way to track your progress, and more than one way to be coached. But at the end of the day, whether you train using power, heart rate, perceived effort, low-tech or high-tech, improving at endurance sports really only comes down to one thing – getting the work down. All of the tech in the world won't push the pedals for you.

CHAPTER 11

Training intensity

Training intensity is one of the most argued-about aspects of triathlon training. In case you hadn't noticed, when it comes to Ironman training I usually fall squarely in the high volume camp, as opposed to the high intensity camp. The reason for my preference is quite simple: when I trained more, I got faster. Sure, when I trained harder, I also got faster, but with a much lower margin of improvement, as we've also seen with most athletes we've coached over the last five years.

In the beginning, when I trained harder I wasn't able to do the volume. Certainly, back in 2011, when I was completely new to the volume required to be competitive enough to race for a Kona slot, I was bound to improve just by training more than I'd ever done before. I was almost guaranteed results simply because it was a completely new type of stress on my body. For an athlete who doesn't have years of volume behind them and who wants to do well at Ironman, volume is the low hanging fruit.

One of the biggest problems I see with athletes' use of high-intensity training is that it stops them doing the volume. The training week of six-time qualifier and twice Kona podium finisher, Alan Ryan (shown in chapter 5), shows sessions where he talks in terms of effort, which ranges from easy, on his five-hour turbo on Saturday, to hard intervals during his one-hour set on Sunday. The thing to note is that Alan isn't sacrificing his next session, or the following day's training, by going too hard during any individual training effort. He knows that consistency is just as important as volume. In fact, without consistency it's pretty much impossible to have enough volume. Another key point is that Alan has years of volume built up and, as a result, his aerobic fitness capacity is massive. He is more than fit enough to handle the increased load of intense and hard sessions without it compromising his overall volume.

Ironman is primarily an aerobic sport and, for most of us, our performance-limiter is either fitness or strength. Speed really only becomes a limiter in so far as we might start too fast and slow drastically as a result. Ironman is also an unusual sport in that the bulk of the participants are in the thirty to fifty age range, yet have an athletic age in single digits, often between one and five years.

For athletes with such a short background in endurance sport, the performance limiter is almost always aerobic fitness and strength endurance. Both of these areas are best trained with a combination of aerobic threshold work and sports-specific strength work. An example would be paddle-and-pull buoy work in the swim, over-geared work on the bike and running heavy, wet cross country or hills.

The aim for me in Ironman training is to be always building a bigger engine, not supercharging a small one. A super-charged Smart car is still only a Smart car; no matter what you do to make it faster it's always going to be limited by its engine size. You might improve its top speed by five or ten percent, but it will be working very hard to maintain that speed.

If you can turn your engine into a big three-litre six-cylinder BMW one, then it will comfortably cruise at those much faster speeds. It might not have the sharpness of a turbo charger but it can go faster for longer and with much more efficiency. Both engines can go relatively fast, but the energy costs of driving at 130 kph in either a Smart car or a three-litre BMW are very different. While the BMW will comfortably cruise at motorway speeds for thousands of kilometres, the Smart car will have to work at much closer to its 'red line' or limit to hold the same speed.

If you can ride at 35 kph at 70–75 percent of your capacity and another rider can ride at 35 kph but is at 95 percent of their capacity, then it's not really rocket science that you will be able to ride at that speed for much longer, with a much lower energy (food) cost. You will also most likely run much better off a bike leg that doesn't overcook you.

Building a bigger engine for Ironman is quite a simple process, but it's not one for which everyone has the patience. It usually requires a lot of time and a high training volume. I know not everyone wants to hear that; we all want to know: what is the quickest way to get the results? But, unfortunately, there aren't really any shortcuts with Ironman.

One of the most respected coaches in triathlon, Gordo Byrn, also believes in volume over intensity and he sums it up really well with the quote:

'People try to short-cut with intensity.' – Gordo Byrn

While he does believe that high intensity or lactate threshold (LT) work delivers results, your LT is rarely the limiter in Ironman:

'While some LT work can be useful, your critical limiter will be steady state aerobic endurance.' – Gordo Byrn

Why is it so important to also be strong for Ironman?

Sports-specific strength is one of the areas that most athletes benefit from. Cycling, in particular, is a strength-based sport where the stronger you are, the bigger the gear you can push and the faster you go.

For example, when you start training let's say that you can ride on a flat road in a 50/18 gear[1] at a cadence of 80 rpm[2] and at a heart rate of 140 bpm, moving at 25 kph. After a period of sports-specific strength training, we usually start to see gains after six to eight weeks, so you might be able to push a 'bigger' gear at the same effort and cadence, which would result in a higher speed. You might be pushing a 50/16 at the same cadence and heart rate, which will result in a faster speed for exactly the same effort.

Another way to think about this is to think about how you would progress in the gym. If your ultimate target was to squat 100 kg, you wouldn't go into the gym on your first day and attempt to just lift 100 kg, you would start with a lighter weight and over days, weeks and months you would gradually add more weight as you get stronger.

---

[1] The numbers refer to the number of teeth on both the chain ring at the front and the cassette at the back. Somewhat confusingly the higher the number at the front the harder the gear but the opposite applies at the back, the smaller the gear the harder it is to push

[2] Cadence is how fast your pedals spin, not how fast you are moving or how fast the wheels are turning

The bike is very similar and the harder gear is like the heavier weight. If you were to go out today and try to ride in the 50/16, you most likely wouldn't be able to turn it for long, but as you get stronger you can push a bigger and bigger gear for longer, resulting in moving faster for the same energy output.

So how do you do sports-specific strength work?

On the bike, the best form of strength work is over-geared or big gear work and this can be done in several ways. When starting off, it's best to introduce the extra load gradually. We do this by including short hill reps. A workout might include the following set.

Example 1

Two-hour ride to include 6 x 3 minutes big gear intervals on a gradual climb. Ride down recovery. Intervals at 70 rpm and 8/10 effort or top of zone three.

Example 2

Two-hour ride to include 6 x 8 minutes big gear intervals on a gradual climb. Ride down recovery. Intervals at 60 rpm and 8/10 effort or top of zone three.

In both examples, you would build up over a number of weeks by lengthening the interval or lowering the cadence. As I illustrated in chapter 5, if you are out for a long, easy ride you can simply put your bike in the big ring and grind away for hours. This is something we tend to give as a session to more experienced and very durable, robust, strong riders so as not to break beginners.

Another favourite of mine is moderately-long intervals on a flat or rolling ride while in the tri bars. This works the exact muscles you will load on race day. An example of this might be:

Example 3

Five-hour ride to include 4 x 20 minutes big gear intervals on flat, rolling terrain. Intervals at 70 rpm and 8/10 effort or top of zone three. Rest of the ride at mid-to-top of zone two at 80 rpm.

How hard is too hard and how do you know where to draw the line?

Phil Maffetone has developed a formula to calculate your AET, or aerobic threshold, which we have also found is almost universally correct. The 'feeling' when you start to train using this as a guide is that it often feels too easy, but in almost every case that we've come across where an athlete sticks with it they see big improvements.

Cillian, a training partner of mine, is one of the strictest followers of the Maffetone Method that I've met and has had spectacular success with it. In his first full season of triathlon and Ironman in 2016, he scored podium finishes in his age group in Challenge Galway, Ironman UK, Ironman 70.3 Dublin and Ironman Wales, not to mention qualifying for Kona, the Ironman 70.3 World Championships and the Challenge Championships.

A very simple way to know if you are training too hard is if you can't finish a planned workout. In these cases, always ask yourself whether you could have finished if you'd gone just a little bit easier.

The inability to finish a training block is another very good indicator of intensity (assuming life or outside stresses aren't the reason). One thing we teach is that what training you do today shouldn't be looked at in isolation, but in relation to how it affects your next session, or the following week's training.

Invariably, I find the first couple of days of a training block feel too easy (and I often try to extend them or add some extra without letting on to Aisling), but that's a reflection of the fact that I'm rested and fresh, not that the training isn't hard enough. Three weeks into the plan, I'm usually getting tired after my over-exuberant start. At that stage I'm wishing I'd followed the plan as prescribed, instead of being impatient and second-guessing my coach. What happens then is that I struggle to complete the more important, harder sessions as I'm fatigued from doing too much earlier in the programme.

Key takeaways

1. Aerobic fitness is the most important aspect of a good Ironman performance.

2. Sports-specific strength is next on the list; being able to push a bigger gear on the bike for the same effort means you are moving faster.

CHAPTER 12

Self-control and pacing

Doing well in Ironman requires self-control, not only in racing but also in training and lifestyle.

1. As we reach the peak of a training cycle, it's very easy to tip ourselves over the edge into over-training. Recognising this and having the discipline to back off when we are often feeling utterly invincible can be nigh on impossible, but at the same time it's a crucial requirement.

2. Having the self-control to train at the correct effort and in the correct zone can also be hard to do. If you're out with stronger athletes, the temptation to push too hard just to keep up and save face is a trap a lot of athletes fall into.

3. The same applies if you're the strongest athlete; there can be the temptation to want to grind everyone else into the ground. This urge is best kept under control until race day...late on race day.

'Mistakes: this is huge for Ironman. How I miss the days when I was the only triathlete with a power meter! The good news is that your competition will (mostly) ignore common sense when they go long. Every group session is an opportunity to maintain peace of mind while others make errors.' – Gordo Byrn

Self-control in racing

This is one of the areas that I love about racing Ironman. It was like discovering the recipe for the secret sauce. It's got less to do with how fast you can go and more to do with how slowly you can force yourself to start. I'll say that again because it's one of the magic bullets. It's got less to do with how fast you can go and more to do with how slowly you can force yourself to start.

During the very early part of the bike in Ironman UK in 2013, I punctured and lost around ten minutes at the side of the road. When I restarted, I had to resist the urge to try to make up the lost time immediately. About five minutes after I got going again, while almost bursting out of myself trying to restrain the urge to push hard, I was passed while going up a slight incline by a guy who looked like a beginner on an entry level road bike. He looked over at me on my fancy tri-bike with the carbon wheels, aero helmet and matching kit and commented that it was a gorgeous bike. He then added that it was a pity I couldn't ride it. He continued to pound the pedals and rode away from me. I was so stunned that I couldn't think of a single smart arse thing to say. Of course, I thought of several funny and smart responses over the next twenty minutes as I stewed over his insult.

I managed to not respond, thinking to myself that I knew how to pace myself and that I'd most likely see him again very shortly, in which case I should stick to my plan. If I didn't catch him, then that was because he was a stronger rider, in which case I still shouldn't chase him.

It only took about twenty minutes for me to catch and pass him as I built into my day and he slowed to a more normal Ironman speed. I'm not the strongest biker, but I do tend to ride at the front end of the age group. When I'm in qualifying shape, I almost always finish with a top ten and often the top five bike split. Despite this fact, in every Ironman I've done I've spent the first twenty to thirty minutes with riders passing me. These were all shapes and sizes, from what looked like beginners to riders that could pass for professionals.

In my first attempt at qualifying for Kona, both Aisling and my coach had told me to start easy, way easier than I thought I should. In fact, what the coach said to me was that I was to go easy for the first fifty kilometres and then I could do what I wanted for the rest of the bike. I could race as easy or hard as I wanted at that point. He said I was to think of it as a 130 km time trial with a 50 km easy warm-up beforehand.

Aisling had an interesting story to illustrate the benefits of self-control and starting easy. Early in her running career she entered her first ultra marathon. The day before the race, she decided to drive the course to see what it was like. It was a 39 mile (63 km) race in the west of Ireland and it took hours to drive the route, which was often on small, mountainous roads. By the time she had finished driving the route, she was even more terrified than before she'd gone out and was almost in tears. If it took hours to drive, how long would it take to run?

At this point, Aisling had never run further than a marathon; this race was 50 percent longer. In her first marathon, she had hit the infamous 'wall' at about 16 miles, what if she hit the wall at 16 miles the following day and still had 23 to go? She could be out there for hours, all day even. She was sick with fear and nerves.

The following morning, at the start of the ultra, she lined up and seeded herself right at the back of the field. Aisling had come up with the idea that she would tell her legs that she was only running a marathon. She would run the first 13 miles so easy that she could pretend to herself and her legs that she was only shuffling an easy warm-up on her way to the start of a marathon. This worked out well from a logistics point of view, as there were three races on the course; there was also a marathon and a half marathon on the same day. The ultra started at mile zero and was 39 miles long, the marathon started at mile 13 of the ultra course and was 26 miles long, and the half marathon started at mile 26 of the ultra. That meant all three shared the same finish line.

All three races started at different times too: the ultra started first, the marathon started 90 minutes later and the half started 90 minutes after that. The faster ultra runners actually caught the slower marathoners and even half marathoners and passed them.

So there she was, running as slowly as she could and at the end of the first mile she found herself all alone in last place. Alone in the wilds of Connemara, but happy that she had a plan. By the time she reached the 13-mile point, she had actually started moving up the field. She was passing runners who had started faster and were now slowing. This was also where she started with the second part of her plan. As I said, she was pretending to herself and her legs that she was only out to do a marathon. So, when she saw the signs for the ultra marathon at the side of the road, she ignored them. Instead, she focused on the marathon ones.

At what was actually mile 13 for her, she started counting as if it was mile one. She didn't want to let the enormity of the task affect her focus or race plan. She would only allow herself to focus on the fact that she now had a marathon to do. She had done a number of marathons before so she could get her head around that much more easily than having to run 39 miles.

All the time, she was catching runners who had started out faster and were now slowing. By the time she reached the final climb, which came in the last five miles, she had moved up to second place in the women's race and was now eighth overall, having also caught and passed almost all of the men. Incredibly, Aisling finished her first ultra in second place and in the top ten overall, despite the fact that at the end of the first mile she was dead last.

So, with that story in mind, I started out the bike way easier than I thought I should and while I didn't quite make it to 50 km before I started racing, I probably rode the first 45 km very conservatively. As a result, I ended up riding a negative split on a course that has more climbing in the second half than the first. In the process, I had one of the fastest bike splits in the age group on the day.

I was under instruction to run the marathon in exactly the same way. I was to do the first ten kilometres way easier than I thought I should. In fact, what Aisling said was to run feeling like I was straining against a leash and had to fight to hold myself back. Again, I didn't quite last the prescribed distance and I started to pick up the pace at about eight kilometres in. As a result of the very conservative pacing plan, I ran the fastest Ironman marathon I'd ever run and improved my previous best overall finishing time by over an hour, on what was a much harder course.

The thing about having that level of self-control on race day is that it's actually very difficult to do. We are probably in the best shape of the year, if not ever. We're rested and fresh for the first time in months. There's the huge excitement that comes from the race itself, which can make reading the signals our body is sending us quite difficult.

Like almost everything else I've talked about in this book, I believe the important thing is to make these mistakes and to learn these lessons in training. Then, when it comes to race day, you're not only in the best shape of your life, but you are much more capable of accessing all of that fitness rather than blowing up and only getting to 70, 80 or 90 percent of your potential.

The next chapters give some examples of how we learn how to race in training.

CHAPTER 13

Process, performance and outcome goals

There are three main types of goals: outcome, performance and process.

The first of these – the outcome goal – is where we want to be, for example, qualifying for Kona or winning a race. This is largely out of our control as we have no influence over myriad factors like who else shows up to race or if we suffer a mechanical failure, crash or just have a bad day.

The second – the performance goals – are what we are trying to achieve, such as racing a sub-ten-hour Ironman. This is also largely out of our control because of factors like weather conditions, wind, heat or high water temperatures, which may mean an unexpected non-wetsuit swim, resulting in a slower time on the day.

The third – process goals – are the only ones that are really within our control. This might be to control our pacing during the early part of the race or to focus on good swim technique. It may even be merely showing up to do a training session to the best of our ability.

Outcome goal

The outcome goal is often the one that drives us initially. It is often also what keeps us going when we are tired, unmotivated or disillusioned with our progress. That big shiny object at the end of the journey, whether it's a finisher's medal, a finishing time, a podium place, a win, a Kona slot or whatever other outcome we desire, is most often the one that keeps us taking steps forward. Until, that is, it becomes the stumbling block that stops us; when that dream outcome starts to look like an impossible ask it can sometimes be the thing that kills all motivation. Even so, outcome goals are useful to drive you forward. The dream of a race win or a personal best (PB) is often very useful to have in training, and can be used as a motivation to train hard or to keep going when you don't particularly want to. These goals motivate you to do the hard sessions that you might otherwise skip because of bad weather, tiredness or just laziness.

Performance goals

Performance goals are what you are trying to achieve. For example, if your aim is to qualify for the Ironman World Championships, you would need to be able to swim, bike and run at certain speeds depending on the course.

To qualify at Ironman UK (IMUK), racing in the 40–44 age group, your overall time might have to be below 10 hours 20 minutes in a typical year. If you were to swim a 1:05, bike a 5:30 and run a 3:30 marathon you should be within that goal, as long as your transition times are quick enough as well and you don't have an exceptionally strong field to contend with.

These targets are all performance goals, allowing competitors to be able to swim, bike and run at a target pace for the duration of the race. However, achieving these performance goals won't necessarily guarantee a Kona slot (or whatever your outcome goal is). In 2011, I finished IMUK in 9:49, which was twenty minutes faster than the last slot won in my age group in the previous year's race. It was also the fastest I had raced in IMUK in three attempts on that course, but it was the only one that I didn't qualify in. For the following two years racing there, I had a slower overall time but, despite that, I qualified both times.

Performance goals are useful to measure our progress and to help us structure our training.

Process goals

Process goals are the ones we have the most control over. In training this might just be to do every session you can; ticking off workout after workout, day after day, is just a process. In racing, a process goal might be to hold back for the first hour of the bike or run, or it might be to hold a good aero position for the entire duration of the bike.

Jocelyn Gardner McCauley, a top-ten finisher in Kona in 2017 and a multiple Ironman and 70.3 champion, spoke in an interview after Kona about how the outcome goal was the one that drove her for months in training. But in the last week before the race she found it more stressful than useful to focus on an outcome goal, so she switched her attention to process goals – things like getting her day-to-day nutrition done to the best of her ability, ticking off the last few training sessions or preparing her bike and kit and planning her race.

For me, Kona was and is the big outcome goal. It's the one that has kept me training and racing for years. But even the most motivated athlete will inevitably have days or weeks, when for whatever reason, that they just don't want to train. At times like these an outcome goal may become stressful and counterproductive. Focusing on a much smaller goal like just getting a day's run done can take the pressure of a huge goal off and allow us to take one more step towards our ultimate aim.

CHAPTER 14

Concentrating on strengths

When I asked experienced competitors what they thought their biggest strength was, a couple of things came up again and again: the first was mental strength, while the second was a strong run or being able to run a strong marathon off a long bike. I could also recognise the humility of these athletes through the answers they provided; most of them told me that they were only average at some, or all three disciplines.

What would you say your strengths are?

Andy Kinnane

'Standalone, probably my run, but I've worked hard on the other two and at this stage I'd say I'm a jack of all trades (might argue master of none also). I think my biggest strength is mental though – being disciplined and making the most of my limited time to train. I'd like to think in a race situation, when things are tough, that I don't give in and always find a way.'

Emma Bilham

'In the grand scheme of things, I'm pretty average at all three disciplines. But I have endurance to compensate for lack of strength. Sometimes my legs will just keep going and I have no idea how. I like tough races and shitty conditions, which I know will faze quite a few competitors. My head can play against me because I constantly doubt myself, but every now and again in races, it shuts up and then it becomes my biggest ally.'

Jocelyn Gardner McCauley

'I am known for my run but would consider myself a bike/runner. Most others would say my strength is mental. I have focused on my mental strength for some time and my favourite books are about sports psychology.'

Garron Mosley

'I'd say I'm good at all three. I'm saying that though because if I could swim, bike or run I wouldn't be doing triathlon – so handy enough at all three to be competitive in a triathlon. I'd say my biggest strength is my belief in my marathon after the bike.'

Emmet Kelly

'With my slowest Ironman marathon at 3:17 and two sub three-hour Ironman marathons, you could say my run. But you have to have a strong bike, holding back all the time, if you want to run a sub-three marathon.'

CHAPTER 15

Facing special challenges...and succeeding

We all make mistakes, in both our racing and training. It might sound very counter-intuitive, but one of the potential downsides of getting yourself in good enough condition to not only complete, but to actually race an Ironman, is that you feel somewhat invincible or superhuman.

Seven- and eight-hour training days, back-to-back training sessions, crushing training partners and just the general feeling of strength and power that comes from being in the best shape of your life can sometimes blinker us when it comes to making the correct decisions.

Here's how two experts, at the top of their game, had to cope with challenges under exceptional circumstances.

What is the biggest mistake you've made in training or racing?

Emma Bilham

'Probably trying to do six half-Ironman races in eight weeks in May–June 2017: two back-to-back, a week's rest, another two, a week off, then the last two back-to-back again. I only made it to number five before realising that the niggle was too big to ignore. I totally underestimated how much the racing, but also the travelling, would take out of me. Making mistakes can be something as simple as forgetting to eat or drink, or thinking that we are going so well that we don't need to. Or it might be that we are so confident that we try something new on race day.'

When taking into account a period of racing in 2017 that included three wins, two second places and a third at six half-Iron distance races, Emma is a perfect example of how when we are flying, we have a tendency to think we are almost invincible. In her case, she clearly was at most races that year, until a minor foot injury put an end to her invincibility.

Here are those results:

1st: Cannes half-Ironman
1st: 70.3 Pays D'Aix
2nd: Bilbao Half Iron
3rd: Ventouxman
2nd: 70.3 Rapperswil
1st: International Triathlon Deauville

Jocelyn McCauley

'I have done far, far too many dumb things throughout this journey. The worst was probably in Kona 2014. I didn't take in any salt during the run because I tried something new on race day. It didn't work, so my electrolyte plan went out the window'

The second part of this story, that Jocelyn is far too humble to tell us about, is that despite running into nutrition issues in Kona in 2014, she went on to win the overall amateur race, taking the amateur Ironman World Champion title in the process.

This further illustrates that the most successful Ironman athletes aren't successful because they do everything right; they are successful **despite** encountering the same problems we all come across in long-distance racing. They just deal with them better than most of us, and they certainly don't let problems stop them from racing to the best of their ability.

CHAPTER 16

On lessons learnt

I asked the athletes what was the biggest lesson they learnt.

Andy Kinnane

'Definitely focus on the process, not the outcome. And really – it's just another race, so do all the things you would in another race at home. Don't let the tanned and ripped show boaters that prance around the expo intimidate you. It's likely you'll be running past them on race day.'

Emma Bilham

'Trust your body, don't listen to your head.'

And, on finishing in second place at her debut Ironman in Nice, France: 'My first Ironman in Nice was a revelation. I had no idea I could do that. I didn't really have the training behind me, but I went into a little bubble and it happened. I've failed to abide by my own advice on numerous occasions since, of course, but it was a real eye-opener.'

Jocelyn McCauley

'When you think of what may happen in the future, you open your mind to fear. In a race, what do you fear? Getting hit in the swim? Not accomplishing your goals? Getting a worse time than before? Not beating so-and-so? All of those things are in the future, they haven't happened yet so what's the purpose of spending energy on them? Stay in the moment, control what you can and the result will be the best you can produce. I think the real fear comes when you think of putting yourself out there and trying your hardest, and then not producing the result you want or think you are capable of. I've done this. It has taken time to be ok with whatever my best is on a certain day.'

Garron Mosley

I've discovered several times that there isn't any way you can 'fluke' an Ironman. Lack of training or preparation, or poor execution will always find you out in a race that is so long and demanding. Garron Mosley rates this as one of the most important lessons he's learnt.

'Honesty, and honesty to yourself. It's very easy to race a 10 km or even an Olympic Triathlon on 75 percent preparation. You can't hide from an Ironman. If you haven't done the work, then don't be disappointed with the result.'

CHAPTER 17

How to learn to race in training

A certain number of your training sessions should be designed not only to deliver a physiological benefit, but also to teach some aspect of racing. That's not to say that there is some magic way to design sessions, some of the lessons best learnt in training are about experimenting and learning things such as pacing, self-control and nutrition – learning how to pace for different distances; learning how much to eat, how much you are capable of eating and how much fuel you need at different intensities; knowing when to hold back, when to push and how much to push; these are all crucial lessons needed to race Ironman effectively.

These objectives should all be incorporated into training sessions in the months and weeks leading up to a race. Because you only get a couple of shots at your Ironman, you want to make as many of your mistakes as possible in training, and then learn from them in order to achieve your true potential under pressure.

Lapped circuits

I had a five-hour ride to do, with long Ironman race pace intervals and Aisling decided to ride with me. At the time we ran at very similar speeds, so we were able to do pretty much all of our running together; swimming at different speeds would just mean choosing the appropriate lane. However, the bike was the one area where there was a considerable speed difference, so for most cycling sessions we had to figure out ways of working around it.

For example, if we had a ride with strength work, we'd ride hill repeats on the same climb at our own pace. This five-hour ride had three times one hour at Ironman race pace. If we did this on a big single loop or an out and back course we would end up thirty kilometres apart by the end. So we decided to do the session on a short lapped circuit because of the speed difference.

Riding on a short lap – the one we chose was 10 km – meant that if I covered 150 km and Aisling covered 130 km, we still wouldn't be more than a few minutes apart if she needed mechanical help, and we could finish at the same time in the same place, regardless of the overall individual distance we covered.

The lapped circuit started out as a way to get around a logistical problem but it ended up being the most important decision we made about that session.

The reason the lapped circuit turned out to be so important was that it eliminated all other variables. With the terrain and weather (wind) constant, if I slowed down it wouldn't be because I had turned back into a headwind or because the terrain was more difficult at the end of the ride, it would be because I had started too fast or not eaten enough.

I also rode the bike on perceived effort: I couldn't use heart rate or power to control my effort. After the warm-up period I started at what I thought 'felt' like the right pace. I averaged just under 37 kph for the first hour and I was almost euphoric. If that was my Ironman pace, I thought, I was in much better shape than I realised and I should pretty much be in qualifying shape already.

I rode easy and ate and drank during the fifteen-minute recovery after the first hour interval. When I started the second hour, I immediately felt different: my legs were starting to feel a bit sore and just a little tired.

'Maybe I did the first one a bit fast,' I thought. 'No problem, I'll just slow down now.' In the second hour, I rode an average speed of 33 kph – still fast enough for a Kona slot at my target race, Ironman UK, which has a hard, hilly, technical bike course where speeds tended to be lower than at faster, flatter Ironman events. However, the effort required to hold that pace was considerably higher. I was also a lot more tired and getting progressively sorer. My breathing was getting harder and I was sweating hard just trying to minimise the drop off in speed.

The fifteen-minute recovery couldn't come quickly enough and again I ate and drank during the short period of easy riding. But as soon as I started into the third hour I knew I was in big trouble. I was really sore and very tired. I couldn't even hold a 30 kph average speed and as I went through the hour I kept slowing more and more. I finished the third interval with an average speed of only 27 kph and was utterly dejected. That was way off Kona qualifying speed for my target race.

Feeling really disappointed, not to mention exhausted, I finished out the session. I was soaked in sweat, sore and hungry and rode what was left of the last hour easy. When I was done, I met Aisling back at the van. We put the bikes away and set out on the 10 km loop for the brick run.

My legs were screaming at me right from the start. My temperature rose and I started sweating heavily again. My back was sore, as were my shoulders. In fact, every inch of me seemed to hurt. How the hell had that happened? I managed to stay with Aisling for about five kilometres, but I was at my limit almost from the start. Aisling on the other hand, who had ridden a more sensible pace on the bike, kept building speed on the run and eventually just cruised effortlessly away from me as I fell apart completely.

By the time I got back to the van Aisling was already getting changed. She had taken more than a minute per km out of me in the second half of the run. That didn't bode well for my first Kona qualifying attempt, which was only four months away. If I extrapolated out the time on the bike, I would have taken almost six-and-a-half hours to ride the 180 km. I needed to ride about an hour faster than that if I was to be anywhere near the required qualifying standard – and I needed to be able to run a marathon off it too.

The next week, I was determined to start slower and, sure enough, my speed was a bit better through the intervals, averaging 34, 33 and 30 kph for each of the one-hour blocks.

On week three, I started a little easier again and had speeds of 32, 33, 33 and more importantly, the effort required to hold a greater speed at the end was much less.

The single biggest lesson I've ever learnt in Ironman is the damage that can be done to your race by even forty minutes of starting too hard on the bike; by starting slower I had not only covered more distance (98 km instead of the previous week's 97 km) in the three hours of intervals, but much more importantly I was speeding up at that point instead of slowing down on the third week.

When I calculated the average speeds from week one and week three for the full 180 km, I ended up covering it in about 05:30 against about 06:15 – that's an incredible 45 minutes difference in just the bike leg, and all because I started the first hour slower. Not because I was fitter (certainly not 45 minutes fitter in three weeks) or that conditions or the course were different (because they weren't), it was all down to pacing.

The other thing that's worth mentioning is that by week three I was not only faster on the bike, but was also running much better off it.

How to maximise your training

1. The first and most important aspect of this session is that it has to be ridden on a short-lapped course. There are two laps we use close to where we live – one is just over six kilometres, the other exactly ten kilometres.

2. The second thing to do is to ride it off feel. You can wear a heart rate monitor for analysis afterwards if you like, but you can neither look at it during the ride nor use it

to pace yourself. The same goes for power – you can record it for analysis afterwards, but you can't use or look at it during the session.

3. You need to use either a watch or bike computer with a lap function (a Garmin is fine) but the only information you can use on it during the session is time, distance, lap speed, lap distance and lap time.

4. I usually warm up gently for twenty minutes by riding to the start of the lap, but you can also start cold as you would on your race day.

The workout

This is the simple part: the standard workout is three times one hour at Ironman race pace (IMRP). If you're a new athlete, or it's early in the season, you might start with three times forty minutes. If you're a more advanced athlete, or it's later in the season, you can build to four times forty-five minutes and up to four times one hour at IMRP. Recovery is ten to fifteen minutes between each interval.

The run is between thirty to ninety minutes off the bike, transitioning as quickly as the climate allows. Pacing is typically a build: starting easy and finishing faster. I usually build on the run to IMRP and rarely run harder than half Ironman pace off this session.

It really sounds too simple to be anything special, but if it's done incorrectly it will kick the shit out of you like you won't believe. When you master it, this will probably be one of the most beneficial sessions you can do.

Why laps?

Because doing this on a lapped course eliminates the variables that can corrupt your results. If you just do this on a big 100 km loop, you don't know if you are slowing down or speeding up due to variables like changing terrain or weather. You might start out with a headwind but finish with a tailwind, so if you start too hard and slow dramatically the numbers won't show this, because your speed later in the workout would be wind-assisted. The same goes for terrain: if you are riding somewhere hilly then unless every lap has the same hills and descents, you won't know if you're holding the same speed throughout the workout.

Why no power or heart rate?

The session is designed to teach you greater awareness of your body and to listen to the signals it sends regarding effort, nutrition, fatigue etc. Learning to read these signals is a crucial aspect of learning to race on feel. Relying on tools to tell you how hard or easy you are going limits your education as an athlete and, much more importantly, you aren't relying on a piece of technology that may stop working on race day.

Power and heart rate individually are very limited in their usefulness. If you are tired or run down, or even if the heat affects you badly on race day, your target power numbers may be too high. Or worse, if you're having the day of your life and you're being held back by a power number, you may throw away the best race you might ever have. If you race with both power and heart rate you are likely to have a more accurate read on the situation. What if one or the other set of numbers is way off on race day?

The problem with using heart rate (HR) in isolation.

Aisling ran her fastest marathon in Rotterdam a couple of years ago. She had trained for it using heart rate and with the guidance of a sports scientist. Over a number of months they had worked out the maximum heart rate she could sustain over the marathon distance so she set out to run at that. The problem was that standing still on the start line, her resting heart rate was at 135. Normally it would be in the sixties or seventies. Within 500 metres of the start line, her heart rate was up over 190. Her target HR for the marathon was 168.

As she stood there, close enough to be able to reach out and touch the elite Kenyan runners, the mixture of excitement, fear and nerves pushed her heart rate so high before even starting, rendering her target numbers meaningless. Instead, she reverted to what she knew best, which was running on perceived effort.

In the end she ran the fastest marathon of her life and she did it with an average heart rate of 182 bpm and a maximum of 199, both of which according to the science and testing they had done before should have been impossible.

Knowing what the correct pace 'feels' like without having to rely on technology is one of the most important skills an athlete can master.

What should happen during the workout?

So, what exactly should happen during this workout that's so educational? Most athletes start the bike leg of an Ironman way too fast; they don't realise just how easy it should feel. For most athletes, including myself, who try this session, the correct pace for the first hour is so easy that it feels almost ridiculous.

I think what happens to a lot of athletes is that they start a little too fast because they are fresh, tapered and rested for the first time in months. They are also probably in the best shape of their lives and can get caught up in 'racing' other athletes around them at the start.

It usually takes forty to sixty minutes for this effort to start to feel a little too hard, at which point they adjust their pace and slow to a more comfortable level. I've also talked to athletes after the race who didn't adjust pacing until hours into the bike, at which point they had completely compromised the bike, the run and their entire race result.

To add extra difficulty to the session, we often ride with athletes of similar or mixed abilities, making the self-control part harder. Again, this doesn't sound like it should affect the workout at all, but in reality it does: riding with others affects how you feel about your pacing. Are you mentally strong enough to allow a rider you know is physically weaker than you to ride away in the first interval? Will you try to ride with him or her from the start, just to save face? Do you trust your own ability and pacing judgement enough to know they will come back to you later in the day? These are the exact decisions you will face in your Ironman and they are the ones that will make or break your day. Learning just how difficult they can be and how to cope with them in training is a key skill for Ironman racing.

Because the session is done on a lap, you all regroup after each interval and early pacing mistakes are highlighted on the second and third block as riders who started too fast blow up or completely fry themselves trying to save face and keep up.

Summary

At the start of the bike when I'm getting passed by people, I remind myself that they are either stronger than me (in that case I shouldn't race them) or they are starting too fast (in which case I still shouldn't race them) and I will see them again shortly. In all races, except Kona, I see almost all of them again as they realise that they have started a little too fast and have to slow down.

CHAPTER 18

Nutrition choices

Practise your nutrition strategy. That's what all the magazine and online articles say you should do. People are advised to practise eating as much as they can on a long ride. Then come race day so many people inexplicably have problems eating what they had in training – so what gives? Why does a strategy that works on every other day of the year suddenly stop working on race day? I think there are a couple of possible reasons.

1. What you eat in the run-up to the race

Some athletes clean up or significantly change their diet in the last couple of weeks before a race, either out of panic or the belief that they will gain some advantage from doing so. Cleaning up what you eat in the last few weeks is ok if that change is an adjustment of what you normally do. For example, cutting out cake or sweets is probably a good idea and is unlikely to harm your race performance. But if you decide to double your intake of water in the last two weeks to make sure you're fully hydrated, you may just succeed in flushing a lot of salts and electrolytes out of your system and harming your race day, rather than helping it.

2. How you 'practise' in training isn't really practice and doesn't relate closely enough to what you do on race day

The mistake I made while preparing for my early races was not eating at my race pace effort. It was only when I started to do long IMRP efforts on the bike that I really started to learn how much to eat and how my body was able to process food at different intensities. I also learnt how much less efficient my body was at IMRP than at easier speeds. I found that my legs would often start to feel sore before I felt hungry. Then when I ate, the soreness went away. It sounds funny and maybe a bit crazy, but that's how it was.

My very unscientific read on it was that the glycogen stores in my leg muscles were becoming depleted and that was somehow causing the soreness. The sports scientists might disagree, but I found that it was a consistent phenomenon. Sore legs, eat, soreness abated (once I'd eliminated the soreness caused by bad pacing, lack of fitness or just fatigue).

I also learnt how much food my body could tolerate at race pace efforts, which I think is one of the most common and costly things we overlook when training for Ironman: if we eat more than we can stomach while racing, it often results in nausea or cramps. If our long, easy bike rides don't include race pace efforts, we will never learn either how much fuel we require at that effort or how much sugar/carbs our stomach can tolerate.

Another lesson I learnt from these sessions was to measure how hungry I was afterwards. If I was starving, then I most likely wasn't getting enough fuel in. If I was ravenously hungry after six hours of training then I would be in trouble in a race lasting ten hours or more. I would either need to eat more, slow down or become more efficient.

3. Pacing during the race

Pacing affects the body's ability to process the food you're eating. If you're racing at an effort that's too hard, then you will burn through your glycogen stores too quickly. Another result of going too hard is that the body may only be able to deal with sending blood and oxygen to the working muscles or to the skin for cooling, and not the stomach to digest the growing pile of sugary energy food accumulating there.

4. Weather conditions

Appreciating how your body's efficiency changes in relation to weather conditions is another point that is often overlooked. Eating as much on a hot race day as you normally do on a cool training day is often very difficult. There's also the extra fluid and salt loss from a potentially higher sweat rate in the heat.

Eating in real life

Nutrition is one of those topics that often cause people to react with an almost religious zeal. There are so many labels – low or high fat, low or high carb, low or no sugar, dairy-free, gluten-free, low salt, unprocessed, vegetarian, vegan and countless more. There are more 'diets' than you can imagine and there as many supporters who will vehemently try to convince you why their way works and all the rest are wrong.

We've tried a couple of these, including high carb, low carb, Paleo and gluten-free and eventually settled on our own 'diet'. It doesn't have a name, but if asked we tend to advise people to just eat real food – food that looks like it did when it fell off the tree, was dug out of the ground or was cut off the side of the animal it originally belonged to. We stay away from processed and fast food, never drink soft drinks, don't drink alcohol (but that's just as much because we don't like the during or after-effects) and don't eat sugar (except occasionally in cake or ice cream). We only use energy products either during a race or in the lead-up to one when we are practising our race day nutrition. And that's pretty much it.

An important point to add is that everyone has different nutrition requirements. What works for me isn't exactly what works for Aisling. I eat more carbs than she does, as well as eating more in general. But I am a foot taller and the best part of twenty kilos heavier. The thing that we believe is universally true is that you should strive to eat real food and never, ever drink soft drinks. We can't understand why anyone would waste some of their daily quotient of calories on a sugary drink. If you're really thirsty, drink water. If you want something sweet, eat cake.

Eating in training

I've spoken about eating in training when practising for race day but what about the rest of the year? We live in a fairly temperate climate so heat is rarely, if ever, an issue in training. So what works for me living in Ireland may not work for someone living in Brazil or South Africa or any place where heat rather than cold prevents training.

What I train with for most of the year is water, bananas, dried fruit, dates or apricots, raw almonds or other mixed nuts – in other words, real food. During almost all of my long steady training I need to stay hydrated and fuelled and I find that real food does that as well as any energy drink, and is a lot healthier than any sugary gel, bar or drink.

However, for hard interval sessions or a long run I do use energy gels or an energy drink, mostly for the convenience and ease of use and also because they work better for that type of session. Almost all other runs are done on empty (especially if it's an easy morning run), as are all swims.

Eating in racing

I think that you should try to stick to what you've practiced in training and be ready to adapt if you encounter unexpected problems. For the most part don't try new stuff on race day.

Energy and sports food and nutrition

Don't believe the hype. Food companies exist to sell food. Bike shops exist to sell bikes. We are both happier when we sell more and you buy more. I don't concern myself too much with what you do with a bike once it leaves the building. You can hang it on your sitting room wall as a decoration or ride it every day. Of course, it's much better if it's ridden regularly, cleaned after each use if needed and it should absolutely live in your house and not in the shed or garden. But really, what you do with it or how many bikes you have doesn't concern me as much as the fact that you're always one bike short of the correct amount. That and the hope that you buy the next one from me, of course.

Food companies similarly don't trouble themselves too much about what happens to the food after it leaves the supermarket shelves. Therefore, if someone's primary objective is to sell more product, you should always treat what they tell you about that product with a pinch of salt (except when you are buying a bike from me, of course – I never exaggerate the benefits of a bike or wheel set).

The claims of performance gains, muscle gains, or any other gains should always be looked at in the context of who is telling you and what *they* have to gain from imparting the knowledge. If the recommendation from the food manufacturer is to take an energy gel every twenty minutes in a race, don't take it as gospel unless you've tried it in training and, just as importantly, tried not doing it too for comparison.

CHAPTER 19

The rules of nutrition

People ask us all the time about nutrition as it relates to sport, health and what we eat in general. I guess they ask me because I'm skinny. At just under six foot tall and usually hovering at around 68 kilos I probably look like I know what I'm doing food-wise. However, it's very important to note that I'm not a nutritionist, neither of us are for that matter, but I guess we have found what works. Or at least what works for us and I think what probably works for most people too.

There isn't anything magic about what we do – we both fall off the broccoli, salad and boiled chicken wagon regularly enough, most often landing face first in something that contains chocolate, or is entirely made of chocolate. But most of what we do is simple, straightforward and sustainable.

Don't mistake simple for easy

If you have problems with food or have eating habits that involve calling out for pizza or burgers more often than boiling up veggies, then making the changes I talk about below isn't easy, but it can be done. Remember, they are just choices, and every one of us has to make these choices every day. The more often we make the right choices, the easier it becomes to make them each day. Eventually those choices just become who we are. Here are some questions you could ask yourself to stay motivated:

- Do I want to eat that cake more than I want to be healthy?

- Do I want to eat that cake more than I want to sleep tonight?

- Do I want to be an athlete or not?

- Do I want that bag of crisps more than I want to be a certain size?

- Do I need to have a soft drink with my lunch?

Our rules of nutrition

In no particular order, below are some of the things that we think are important when it comes to food. These are not hard and fast rules – they are just what we do. They work for us and they may work for you too.

1. The Pareto principle says that if 80 per cent of what you eat is good, then 20 percent can be bad(ish). It should probably be 90/10, but I'm not always that disciplined.

2. There is no magic 'diet' – just eat real food!

3. Eat lots of salads. I was lucky enough to grow up in a family that ate salads regularly, so I acquired a taste for them as a kid. The important word there isn't 'salads', it's 'acquired'. I probably didn't pop out of the womb craving a carrot or a pickled onion, but that was what we ate when I was growing up, mostly in the summer. I guess I just grew to like them. Despite the bad press, salads aren't the most boring food on the planet, quite the opposite – you just need to be a little inventive.

4. When you decide to deal with food and nutrition it needs to be sustainable. Going on an 'Onion Soup Only' diet for six weeks and losing 27 kilos so you can fit into your wedding dress or suit isn't really sustainable. What are you going to eat when you stop eating the onion soup? Broccoli and carrots? Or will it be back to the Big Mac that you normally have for dinner? Onion-flavoured water is not a sustainable food choice for the rest of your life – you need to eat as long as you're planning on being alive. So it's best if you choose to eat real food that you enjoy and that won't kill you.

5. We don't usually eat three meals a day: it may be two meals or five, depending on how much or how hard we're training. Three meals a day is a product of modern society and the way our lives are structured around work or school. Eating when you're hungry is a better guide to how much and when you need to eat, but may be skewed if you eat a lot of processed or sugary foods, as these often have the side effect of causing cravings that feel like hunger.

6. I normally don't eat before training in the morning, but if a session is long or hard I will eat both during and afterwards. Almost every nutritionist I've ever spoken to disagrees, but traditional nutritional thinking isn't really working. We are becoming a planet of overweight, sick people.

7. We don't use supplements unless prescribed them by a doctor.

8. I don't use recovery products unless I'm losing weight uncontrollably due to a very high training load and I physically cannot eat enough to halt the weight loss. I eat real food after training. That means no protein shakes, bars, tablets or anything else that comes out of a bottle, tub or jar.

9. Food should look like it did the day it was pulled from the ground, picked off the tree or sliced off the side of the animal it belonged to. It should not come delivered in a box, bag or wrapper.

10. We don't drink alcohol.

11. We don't drink soft drinks...ever. Ok, except maybe for a coke during an Ironman marathon.

12. We do eat cake...regularly. Probably I eat it too regularly, to be honest.

13. The amount of food we eat is dependent on the volume of training we do. When we are in heavy training, we eat more. When we are only ticking over and exercising lightly we need less, therefore we eat less.

14. We eat almost no processed food.

15. What processed food we do eat is usually the treat – i.e. cake.

16. We cook or prepare most of our own meals.

17. I try to limit my indulgence of items on the banned list to one a day. This makes me choose carefully. If I can only have one treat then it certainly won't be a cheap bar of chocolate. It will most likely be something I really

like – something for which it's worthwhile taking a trip off the reservation.

18. We rarely use energy drinks, gels or bars in training. As much as possible it's water, fruit, nuts or dried fruits. However, we do use energy products while racing and during the last couple of months in the lead in to a big race to establish how much we need to eat and drink and whether or not we are able to stomach it. We also find they work well for long and hard sessions.

19. Over time I've learnt to limit my caffeine intake, and my last coffee is usually at lunchtime. I find if it's any later it disturbs my sleep. I really noticed this when my training volume ramped up and recovery and sleep became much more important.

20. I do the same with sugar. If I'm having that sweet treat it's usually early in the day. It was a real eye opener for me to learn that sugar has a similar effect on my sleep as caffeine.

21. I don't limit the amount of food I eat: I eat until I'm full. I don't think I've ever met someone who has become overweight eating chicken, potatoes, fish or vegetables. Real food has a built-in stop button, fake food doesn't. You usually stop eating real food when

you're full; you reluctantly stop eating Jaffa cakes when they're gone. They have no stop switch.

22. Sometimes food is invisible. I was in work chatting to Aisling the other day and remarked that I was starving. She answered that there wasn't anything unusual about that. I replied that I hadn't had anything to eat all day. She then asked me about the Danish pastry and coffee I'd had on the way into work that morning; I'd forgotten all about it. I think of these little snacks as invisible food. We don't really count them and often forget them altogether. I'd had a cake for breakfast and forgotten all about it.

23. While we are on the subject of Danish pastries and croissants, pastries are cakes. They might be as light and fluffy as little clouds but they are still cakes.

24. Coffee shouldn't have marshmallows, syrup, sugar, chocolate sprinkles or sweetener in it. Coffee is coffee. If you want all that other shite, stop messing around and just have a cake.

25. We eat full fat everything. Butter, cream, milk, cheese. If they've taken the fat out, they've put some other shite in instead – usually some sort of sugar. If you want the sugar, stop lying to yourself and see point 15 or 24.

26. Training a lot is not a licence to eat anything I want, although for years I thought it was.

I think that making wholesale changes to what we eat all in one go is unsustainable; changing one thing at a time is the best way to make things stick.

How to get started with your nutrition.

Start with an honest food diary. Detail everything you eat and when. Everything – all of it. It will probably shock you. It certainly shocked me the first time I did it. Using the food diary, make a list of the things that you want to change, or that you think are wrong with your current eating habits. It might look something like this:

1. Eating sweets twice a day.

2. Drinking soft drinks.

3. Eating service station or deli food in the car during the commute.

4. Having marshmallows in coffee.

5. Drinking wine with dinner each day.

6. Drinking pints at the weekend.

7. Ordering in most meals.

8. Eating biscuits and drinking tea every night.

We all have vices. Mine (as you may have guessed) are chocolate and cake or, more accurately, chocolate biscuit cake. That and ice cream, or chocolate cake and ice cream. Controlling these weaknesses is just part of the journey to better nutrition.

Once you've completed your food diary and made a list of the problem areas you want to address, the next step is to number them in order of importance. I start with the biggest potential gains at the top of the list (the low hanging fruit) and continue all the way down to the lowest gains. I would then aim to fix just one thing a week. The first week you might decide not to eat any takeaways or fast food. The second week you might stop drinking soft drinks. The third week you might cut out the marshmallows in your coffee.

Of course, you may say that these are all easy to list out and suggest how to fix, while I sit here all fit and skinny. But I too had all of those issues at one stage or another. I smoked up to sixty cigarettes a day and thought I'd never be free of them. I drank too much when I was in my twenties. I ate all the rubbish, all the time and thought that because I trained a lot I could get away with it.

The biggest problem with eating bad food is that feeling bad all the time becomes our default norm. I had no idea that I was meant to feel any other way until I eventually cleaned up my eating. When you eat well, you feel good and realise just how big an impact that rubbish food has on your whole life. When I changed my nutrition habits I wasn't tired all the time. I stopped having stomach and digestion issues and my moods were better. I slept better and, as a result, trained and worked better.

The instant feedback of sleep

Sleep is one of the things that keeps me honest. If I eat too much rubbish then I don't sleep well. If I were to wait for the feedback of having put on weight, that would take weeks or months, and weight gain can be so insidious and gradual that it's easily ignored. The effect on my health is even more gradual and invisible and, as a result, it's even easier to push those thoughts aside. However, if I don't sleep, it has an immediate impact on my training, my mood, my work and my life in general. I know that food, sugar and caffeine in particular affect me most in this area so I get the instant, painful feedback that I'm screwing up and I am more likely to review my junk food intake to fix it.

Takeaways (not the kind you get in a paper bag at the chipper)

1. Start with a food diary.

2. List all the changes you want to make.

3. Pick the most impactful ones first – the low-hanging fruit.

4. One change a week – don't try to fix everything at once.

5. Eat real food.

6. Diets don't work.

7. Don't screw around with your coffee.

8. It's alright to eat cake – just not all the cake, and not all the time.

9. Whatever you try, it has to be sustainable. Stay away from magic onion-flavoured water crash diets. Can you live with eating what you're planning on eating during your 'diet' for the rest of your life? If not, you're only fooling yourself.

10. You most likely don't need that recovery shake. In fact, I could almost guarantee that you don't need it.

11. We are always looking for balance. It's alright to treat yourself, but it's important to recognise what a treat is:

the Danish pastry, the wine, the burger, the crisps are all treats. They shouldn't be considered food. Try to limit treats to one a day.

CHAPTER 20

Sacrifice or investment?

Back in 1999 I read a book by a guy called Alan Carr that changed my life. It was called *The Easy Way To Stop Smoking*. I was a voracious reader at the time. Not doing triathlon, or any sports for that matter, meant I had lots of spare time available for reading.

I normally read reasonably quickly and would typically get through a book in anything from a couple of days to a week or two at worst. This book, however, took me three months to finish. It wasn't a hard read, but it was written to change lives and I could feel it working on me and I decided that I wanted to hang on to my cigarettes as a crutch for just a little longer. As much as I wanted to be free from cigarettes, I had smoked for over a dozen years and a part of me was afraid of what the loss of them and the resulting change would bring.

I started reading the book in the first week of January. It was after another Christmas of not only eating and drinking too much, but also smoking too much. At the time I was smoking two to three packs, or forty to sixty cigarettes, a day. I started every day with a cigarette. The minute I woke up I reached for the pack beside the bed and lit one up immediately. This started off my coughing, which resulted in me hacking up brown or green phlegm. It was the most disgusting way to start your day and I hated it. I was out of breath just walking briskly and a flight of stairs would kick off another coughing fit.

Another holiday season of feeling even worse than usual, because of the effects of the cigarettes being amplified by my daily hangover, drove me to look for a way to stop smoking. Over the years I'd tried lots of the other ways: willpower, nicotine patches or gum and more. I was wandering through a bookshop when I saw Carr's book and I decided to try it. I didn't really hold out much hope, but I decided to try anyway. I'd reached the point of needing to do something…anything.

I finished the book on 17th March 1999 and smoked my last cigarette. At that point, according to Carr, I immediately became a non-smoker. One of the cornerstones of Carr's idea was that 'giving up' anything carried an air of sacrifice and sacrifice needs willpower to sustain it. As a result it was almost always doomed to failure. After countless previous failed attempts at 'giving up' smoking I had to agree.

Instead he imbued the idea of being a non-smoker with a sense of empowerment and self-control. This, in itself, provided me with huge motivation. You could easily have a weak moment and slip backwards if you felt like you were denying yourself something that at times could offer comfort. But if you were gaining self-satisfaction and empowerment from being a non-smoker then you didn't have to fight that sense of loss or sacrifice. Any cravings I still had were just reminders of all of the positive things that being a non-smoker brought along with it.

Looking at being a non-smoker as a positive thing, and never seeing it as denial or sacrifice was one of the things that guaranteed my success. It's also the way I see my training. Being a triathlete is empowering and positive. It's not something that I have to make sacrifices to be. I don't see it as sacrifice. I never did. I always thought that we are incredibly fortunate to be able to do what we do. Very few people can live a life chasing their dream and I always thought that it would be very selfish to think of anything I had to do, or not do, in pursuit of my dream as a sacrifice.

If you were to start a business and had to put some of your own money or time in to make it grow and become successful, you would most likely see it as an investment not a sacrifice. I think of any of the things I do to try to become a better athlete in the same way. Going to bed early so I can train in the mornings now is just what I do. Rarely, if ever, do I resent not being able to go out at night. Rather, it's a positive choice that I make.

Choices are positive and are much easier to live with than sacrifices. Sacrifices always sound hard, unfair, like something I'd rather not have to do. They make me feel like a martyr. Choosing to live in a way that allows me to swim, bike and run like I do is not a sacrifice. Swimming, biking and running are the things we do for fun. They are playing. We might take Ironman and the whole Kona thing very seriously, but it's important to remember that being able to do this is a privilege and, as long as I can physically continue to swim, bike and run, I will continue to remind myself of that.

That's not to say that it's easy or that I never just want to go to the movies and eat a big pile of popcorn and sugary rubbish. In that instance, I would make a choice. I would either decide that I wanted my long-term goal more than the instant gratification, or I would decide to eat the cake.

I heard Olympic triathlon champion, Gwen Jorgenson, in a podcast interview after the Olympics being asked about all of the sacrifices she had made to get where she was. She replied to it in a way that I thought put into words perfectly what I felt but had never articulated as well. She said that she never saw what she did as a sacrifice – whether it was missing social events, going to bed early or being careful about what she ate. She saw everything she did as an investment in herself, her career and her goals.

She went on to make the point that if we put away a portion of our salary each month into a savings account we don't feel like we are sacrificing that money, rather that we are investing it for our future. That was how she looked at her training.

I thought it was the perfect way to think about it. After all, how long can you go on doing something you see as a sacrifice? How long can you go on doing something that is ultimately stopping you doing something else? It's much easier to stick with something if you see it in a positive light and see it as adding to the quality of your life.

CHAPTER 21

On overcoming adversity

Almost universally, Kona qualifiers deal with adversity better than most athletes. When I asked what sort of problems they encountered and overcame either during, or in the build-up to a race, most had a story of qualifying or winning despite having problems in a race that would have most of us thinking that our day was over.

What was the hardest thing you've had to overcome in a race or training?

Andy Kinnane – Kona 2017

Andy spoke about his 2013 season and the problems of being injured for months before Ironman Austria, and not being able to run at all in preparation for it.

'In 2013, when I had injury problems and spent more time in the gym and on a Pilates mat than running, I had a great coach who gave me confidence that what I was doing was the right thing to do for me at the time.'

It's worth mentioning here that, despite not being able to run in training in the lead-up to this race, Andy still managed to run a PB at Ironman Austria and, in the process, went under ten hours for the first time.

Emma Bilham

I was really surprised with Emma's answer to this question. For a professional triathlete to be afraid of something that almost every one of us also fears was unexpected, especially after seeing Emma swim. She would lap me several times whenever she was in the pool at the same time.

'The swim start, every single time – especially if it's a beach start and everyone goes off together. I'm not big enough to run through water so I have to swim when everyone else is still running. I get battered, and it scares the shit out of me.'

'Maybe also the asthma attack which hit me 150 km into the bike leg of Embrunman in 2016. It was 35 degrees and suddenly I couldn't breathe, couldn't eat, couldn't let my heart rate spike or I would have to stop to cough my guts up. I finished the bike and somehow got through the run on water and oranges. I was on oxygen for two hours after. But I finished the race and it showed me how many reserves my body really had.'

Jocelyn McCauley – age group race winner before turning pro and making a top ten Kona female professional finish

Jocelyn's answer, like Emma's, illustrates that there is rarely a race or build up to one that is without adversity or difficulty, and that it's the athletes who deal best with these situations who will most often have the best results.

'While training for my first Ironman I had my first bike crash, about three weeks before the race. I broke a rib and had some nasty road rash. I was out of the pool till race week and did two short swims. I was so worried that I would get kicked in the chest since it was still a mass start then with over 2,000 athletes.'

'My first Ironman win I crashed pretty badly three days before. I had nasty road rash for the race but was fine other than that.'

'Last year (2017) at IMTX I needed to get thirteenth to have enough points for Kona but was predicted to win the race. I ended up getting three flats. I repaired the first one, I got a new wheel for the second and I had amazing age groupers stop and give me things for the third. After that third flat, I was stuck in my hardest gear for the last half of the bike. I did end up finishing, but in twelfth place.'

Garron Mosley

'I'm very lucky. Because most of my training is at very low intensity I'm able to recover well. I've had very little injury worries other than self-inflicted problems. I missed the whole of the 2012 season due to a bad bike crash, but that was my own fault. I think picking myself up and getting back into things was difficult, but the simple fact that I was able to ride a bike again was enough motivation in itself.'

CHAPTER 22

On developing patience

It's a bit ironic that I'm here writing about having patience when I tried to qualify for Kona the first time on five months training, and not the twenty-four I'm telling you it typically takes.

When we set out with a target to do our first race, be it a triathlon, a running race, an Ironman or whatever the challenge, most of us allow a certain amount of time. It might be four, six or maybe even twenty weeks to get fit and complete the event.

Often our next target is to get faster, so we go back, and again we allow ourselves a certain amount of time to get in shape. Sometimes we add in extra training and maybe do some intervals or other specific sessions. This usually works for a while and we get faster, and then along comes the big idea: I wonder, could I podium in my age group? Win a small race? Break a certain time for a distance? Qualify for Kona? Or whatever else our target is.

It's often a stretch from where we currently are, so when we decide to go for it, we train like crazy. This might involve harder, faster, longer sessions and sometimes it works but often it doesn't and, as failure looms, we stop and accept defeat.

But what if the only thing we are getting wrong is the amount of time it takes? What if we allowed ourselves longer – much longer – to reach the big goals? Instead of thinking about how we could cram in ten weeks of training for an event, what if we managed to do a little less each week, but trained consistently in a sustainable manner for one hundred weeks?

Can you even begin to imagine how much fitter, faster, stronger or healthier you would be if you were able to sustain a training block for 400 weeks? If training properly and consistently became a lifestyle and a normal part of your life?

I listened to Bryan McCrystal, the current Irish Ironman record holder, being interviewed on a local radio sports show, and when he was asked how he broke the Irish Ironman record not once, but twice, in 2015, he answered by going back to when he started in triathlon in 2007 or 2008.

He trained, raced and learnt for the previous eight years (let's not forget that before that he played professional football for Leeds United in Britain, so he's actually been in sports at a very serious level for about twenty years). You could say he's just your typical overnight success. It only took him about 400 weeks to become the athlete he is now and, at the time of writing, the best in the country.

Years ago, while talking to another elite triathlete we sponsored, I asked him what his targets were in the sport and he answered by telling me where he saw himself in a month, six months, a year, two years and more. I was stunned that he thought about his sport the way I thought about my business. I know where I want to be with it in one, two or three years but I also have daily, weekly and monthly targets to hit along the way. Back then, I'd never come across someone who thought about triathlon, and more particularly Ironman, in that way.

I know that since I started my business, the things that I thought were my limits have all changed. Twenty years ago, numbers that I thought of as monthly sales targets are now often daily ones. I've had months in business where my sales were bigger than my first year's total sales. I wouldn't have believed that was possible if you had told me back in 1998. I simply wouldn't have been able to comprehend how my small business could grow to that level.

The limits we set ourselves are only the limits of our current reality, or the limits of how far in the future we can imagine. If we dream big, we have to allow that it will take time to become something that is, right now, way beyond our reach. When I first set out with the dream to qualify for Kona, I was so far away from that reality that it looked impossible to everyone (including both my coach and myself at the time). Everyone, that was, except Aisling. When we started, we aimed to do it in less than six months but I knew that if I didn't make it first time out, that I would keep going for twelve, eighteen or twenty-four months if that was what it took.

I think one of the most important things to learn about improving and becoming good at Ironman is that it can take a long time. If you really want to succeed at Ironman, age and talent aren't the limiters (thankfully for me on both counts), so stop thinking about being in a hurry and only giving yourself five, ten, fifteen or twenty weeks to become faster. Think not only about this year's race, but about next year, and the year after that. Imagine how much you could improve by training consistently for the next 400 weeks.

Then think about how much you would have to slow down in your training so as not to burn yourself out. How careful would you have to be with your pacing and effort so that you can train every week?

When we look further than today's training to next week's or next month's then we can approach the sessions a little differently. If I know that I have fourteen hours of hard hilly biking in the programme this week, then I'll make sure that I don't fry myself on the long interval run on Thursday. I want to get all of the training done, not just the one epic session. I want to make sure that I can finish out the current training block without needing to take extra rest days because I've overdone a couple of sessions.

I always try to look ahead: what effect will today's decisions have on tomorrow's, or next week's training? What effect will training through an injury have next week, next month or in the longer term? Obviously, I didn't always think like that. See the story about my legendary status back in Chapter 10.

But if we want to make big changes, it takes time. In my case it took a lot of time.

CHAPTER 23

Good guidance is crucial

Find the best, most successful teachers and learn all you can from them.

For me, finding someone who knew what was required to become a Kona athlete and getting their guidance was crucial. I was not only coming from a non-endurance-training background but I also had no idea what to do or how to go about it. If I had tried to go it alone and figure out what to do myself, I would likely have been so far off the mark that I would have eventually come to the conclusion that it simply wasn't possible for me to qualify.

Even if I had the strength and conviction at the time to keep on going and figuring it out for myself, it would have taken considerably longer. But to be honest, I think that my idea of what was required before I started out was so far off the mark that I'm not sure that I would have been successful at all.

So, in the absence of knowing what to do, we went out and found a coach. I like to tell the story about our first conversation with him: I told him that I wanted to try to qualify for Kona. I added that I wanted to do it later that year – about nine months later to be exact. His immediate answer was that it wasn't possible. I wouldn't qualify and certainly not in that short space of time. Maybe if I allowed myself two full years, but even then it was unlikely that I would make it. He didn't think I was Kona material.

I was really disappointed but I'm nothing if not resourceful (or even stubborn), so I immediately replied with a question. 'Do you know how to coach someone to qualify for Kona if they have the ability?'

'Yes of course,' he said.

'Ok so give me that plan. Coach me as you would someone who was capable of qualifying. I'll take full responsibility if you break me or if it doesn't work.'

He looked at me dubiously but reluctantly agreed.

My training volume jumped from the six to eight hours a week I was currently doing, to over thirty hours. Incredibly, I got faster immediately. I raced just over a week later and won my age group for the first time ever, placing third overall.

That was at a sprint triathlon. Bear in mind that I was training for Ironman and I had just done as much training in the previous week as I'd managed most months that year. In theory, I should have been fried, but instead I raced faster than I'd ever

148

done before. The fried part would come later, but for the moment I was flying.

Anyway, back to the coach. It never would have occurred to me in a million years to increase my training from six to thirty hours a week all in one go. Even if it had, I never would have had the confidence to attempt it, it simply sounds ludicrous. I also wouldn't have had the knowledge of what to do. Taking on a coach allowed me to improve in ways I only could have dreamed about . It also allowed me to do that in a massively accelerated manner.

The coach we worked with was one of those people who, once committed to something, was willing to push the boundaries way past what most others would risk. In taking on the challenge of getting me to Kona, he knew he would have to push me past any limits that I'd reached before, and every time I reached a new limit he would push again.

One of the first things he said to me once we got started was that I hadn't got a chance of qualifying at Ironman Florida, which was the race I'd chosen. It was a race that would exploit all of my weaknesses. I was a relatively weak swimmer and, at 68 kg, was fairly light for my height, an unfortunate quarter inch under six feet. As a result I was reasonably good on hills on both the bike and run. Florida had a challenging sea swim and pancake flat bike and run courses, so any power-to-weight advantage I had on a hilly course would be negated. It was also likely to be hotter than I was used to. If I were to have any chance at qualifying, I would have to pick a race with a more suitable course and weather conditions.

At the coach's suggestion, we switched to Ironman UK, which had a hilly and hard bike and run and an easy lake swim. All of which suited me much better. The weather was also likely to be more temperate and suited to someone from Ireland who didn't race as well in the heat. The only drawback was that it was four months earlier, leaving me just under five months to go from just inside the top 1,000 at my last attempt, to somewhere inside the top fifty. So an impossibly tall order just got taller.

The coach brought me the confidence to push the limits but also – and probably more importantly – he taught me. He taught me how to do my nutrition correctly and the importance of both bike and run pacing. He taught me some aspect of how to race Ironman in almost every training session.

By the time Aisling took over my coaching we had both spent several years learning about what did and didn't work. Aisling learnt a lot quicker than I did. She is what I would call an instinctive coach. Not relying on power meters or stopwatches, she taught me to race and train on feel. My fastest Ironman results came when not using a watch, heart rate monitor or power meter, but racing on perceived effort.

With Aisling coaching me now, I'm in the very fortunate position that she can react and adjust my training daily if needed. She also knows exactly how much stress I'm under with work or any other external situation and can factor this into the programme in a way that almost no other coach could possibly do.

Coaching was probably the most important aspect of my initial Kona journey. It accelerated my physical progress and my learning in a way that I never could have done alone. Now, having Aisling coach me allows me to hand all that responsibility to her and allows me just to focus on doing what I'm told. It allows her to make training decisions pragmatically and without the emotional baggage I might bring to it because I'm so invested in the outcome. Because of training fatigue and my drive I don't always make good decisions.

I know that coaching isn't something that is available to everyone. Maybe it's because of the prohibitive cost, access to coaches or lack of coaches available in an area. However, there are other ways to learn how to train to qualify. A mentor is the next best option, but be sure to choose yours carefully. They needn't have qualified themselves, but they must know how to qualify. Of course, there's also the internet. There is no end of blogs, magazines and websites telling you how to do it, but again choose your sources carefully.

CHAPTER 24

Overcoming your fears

If you waste your time humming and hawing in a given situation, someone else is going to make the choice for you. And most likely, you won't like what they choose. It doesn't matter if you don't know how to get where you want to go. Once you start working towards a goal, you can alter your direction en route. If you wait until you can see how to take every step of the journey, then you will never start.

Back in 2010, we were faced with a huge and very scary choice. Aisling and I ran our own business. It was a small bike shop in a 700 square-foot unit in a local shopping centre. We knew the business had the potential to be much bigger, but it was restricted by the tiny space it occupied. At the same time, that small, comfortable world was safe and somewhat profitable. Moving was a risk, and the risk was substantial. Our entire household income came from that small shop. If the move wasn't successful, the repercussions could be disastrous. There was still the desire to allow it to grow, but to do that we would have to find a bigger unit.

We looked at shops that were double our size at the time and we were full of ideas of the things we could do with more space. Even doubling up didn't seem like it'd be enough. So we continued looking for a bigger space.

Not long after we started searching, I got a phone call from a very good friend who said he had a large retail unit that he thought would be perfect for us. We hadn't told anybody that we were looking at expanding, but that was one of those opportunities that sometimes just fall out of the sky and land in your lap.

I went to look at it. It was locked up when I arrived so I cupped my hands against the glass and peered in through the huge dusty windows. It was over 8,000 square feet and our existing store was less than one tenth of that size. As I peered in the window, I couldn't imagine how I could possibly ever get from being a tiny local business to what could be the biggest bike shop in the country, all in one step. How could I even fill a store that was ten times as big? Where would I get that much money, or the staff, and how could I pay the rent? I was so terrified by the size and scope of the project that I got back in my car and drove away.

Aisling and I talked about it again that evening, but we couldn't see a way to make it happen. And probably, more importantly,

I was too afraid to try it – which was something I would not admit to Aisling or anybody else. Who wants to admit that they won't do something because they are too afraid?

But we still had the same problem when we went back to work the next day. Where we were was driving us crazy. It was causing us to lose business and stopping us expanding into areas we knew we were missing out on. So we continued to look for another option. The seed had been planted. I only dreamed of the big shop. I imagined all we could do with that much space. We could have the biggest and best specialist triathlon shop in the country. I just couldn't get that dream out of my head.

The internal conflict of the desire to grow and the fear of the unknown and possible catastrophic failure came to a head a couple of months later. As usual, it was something Aisling said that made me take action: 'You'll never forgive yourself if someone else does it before us. If someone else opens that huge shop in Dublin and you miss the opportunity, you won't be able to live with it.'

I knew she was right, so we decided to go back and look at the big space again.

A couple of days later I sat down with the landlord. I still had no idea of how I would make it happen, where the money would come from or how we would stock it. Despite all of that we went ahead and signed a lease on it. That meeting with the landlord went on until 1 am.

I drove home on an emotional rollercoaster. One minute I was feeling so excited at the prospects that I thought I might burst, the next I was swallowing down the urge to vomit as a wave of fear and panic hit, when the enormity of what I'd just agreed to do hit home.

I climbed into bed beside Aisling trying not to disturb her and at the same time hoping that she was awake and waiting to hear how it went. She turned over as I slipped in beside her and asked how it had gone. I told her I'd agreed a deal and we'd have the keys the following week. She mumbled that that was good and promptly fell back asleep.

The next morning in the clear light of day Aisling described that moment as feeling like we were stepping blindly off the edge of a cliff, without knowing what was below or how far we might fall and without the comfort of a parachute to save us if things went wrong.

Now don't get me wrong. We didn't just decide on an impulse to make the leap. In the preceding months, we had researched all we could about any other big successful stores like the one we hoped to build, travelling to the UK and Europe to look at similar businesses to what we wanted to build and talk to the owners. I'd spent months writing business plans. I'd written dozens of sales projections and profit and loss spreadsheets, looking at where the break-even point was, what the minimum we needed to do to make it successful was and how badly could it all go wrong if it didn't work.

But in all such situations there comes a point where you need to make a decision. As the first accountant I ever worked with told me as he taught me how to write a business plan: 'Paper won't refuse ink and you can make projections saying anything you want.' All the planning and research in the world aren't worth anything if you never actually take that vital first step. There comes a point where you either believe in something or you don't – where you either decide to do something, or you don't.

In the end, for me, it was probably the fear of losing out on what might be a once-in-a-lifetime opportunity that forced me to step up and make the difficult decision. It was when the fear of missing out on that opportunity became bigger than the fear of failure, that I was forced into action.

If you wanted to drive across the country, you wouldn't wait until every set of traffic lights was green. You probably wouldn't even open a map before you started. You would just get in your car, switch on the GPS and trust it to direct you there. Trying to anticipate every problem you might encounter and preparing for it before you started would only stop you from ever starting. Sometimes you just have to jump in and start, and deal with delays and problems as you go.

I think Google or Facebook has a saying that goes: 'Done is better than perfect'; it's easy to improve something that exists, but impossible to fix something that doesn't.

So, we opened the big shop and the learning curve was absolutely savage. It wasn't steep – it was vertical. All of a sudden, making mistakes cost tens of thousands of Euros, not hundreds. Over the next three years we made lots of those very expensive mistakes and, very gradually, over time, we made the new business profitable. But it took years, not weeks or months.

Despite the fact that I couldn't possibly see how to do it before we started, taking that first step was the most important one. We have changed direction plenty of times as we have made mistakes and learnt from them, but none of them was as important as taking that first step – taking that plunge, committing, and not having a safety net or parachute, makes a person almost desperate to succeed. When the alternative is catastrophic failure, there really is no other option but to make plans work and to figure out how to translate them into reality.

So, fear can be a huge motivator as well as a limiter. It's up to us to decide which one we allow it to be.

CHAPTER 25

Turning dreams into reality

I'm of the opinion that belief in a dream is far less important than the willingness to just begin working towards it. Dreams don't just fall out of the sky and land in your lap. They are built one step, one workout, one day at a time.

I also don't necessarily think that you need to fully believe in a dream to start taking steps towards realising it. That might sound a bit crazy, but that's how it was for me when I started to try to qualify for Kona. I wanted it, I dreamt about it, and I tried to believe it was possible, but really, for the first five months, I never believed it deep down; I never felt like a 'Kona person', at the beginning of my journey.

Aisling was the one who believed it was possible, and I trusted her. In the beginning her belief in me was enough to convince me to start. One of the other things that convinced me to start was the experience I spoke about of successfully expanding our business to a size that I couldn't really wrap my head around when it was small.

I think I knew that belief wasn't a requisite to getting started. The first time I actually believed that I could qualify was during my first attempt at Ironman UK in 2011. I was coming to the end of the bike leg and I caught and passed a professional female who had started the race as the favourite. As I went by and saw her name on her race number I almost fell off my bike with surprise. I knew that the top age group men would be racing with or ahead of the professional females. This was the first indication that I was actually where I dreamt of being.

A couple of kilometres later, I rolled into an almost empty transition area and again was struck by the realisation that I was actually doing it. That was the first time I really believed that I could realise my dream. During the months leading up to the race I was trying to believe that I could qualify, but there was so much self-doubt in the first few months that it never really stuck.

If I'd allowed that doubt, or lack of belief in my ability to do it, to decide my course of action, I never would have started. One of my biggest realisations was that when it comes to Ironman, there's a certain inevitability about just doing the work.

Luckily for me it is a sport that rewards a lot of hard work and doesn't require huge, freaky genetic talent. Aisling says that sometimes you have to 'fake it till you make it.' In other words, by simply doing the work and acting like a Kona person for long enough, you will inevitably become that person.

CHAPTER 26

The benefits of marginal gains

Plenty has been written about the benefits of marginal gains, as the idea has been popularised by the Team Sky professional cycling team. I've written myself about the subject a number of times before, on my blog. I think that although the biggest part of getting fast comes from just doing the hard work, there are lots of additional gains to be made by also looking after the smaller details. Often these are very much the 'one percenters', but if you add enough of them together, along with the big gains made from training (the 90 percent), they can sometimes be the difference between a podium, hitting a time target or a Kona slot. But at what point does chasing these small gains become ridiculous or even a liability?

When I first decided to chase a Kona slot, I made the decision that if I was going to put in all of the work and investment required to qualify, I wasn't then going to miss out on a Kona slot by one or two minutes because I hadn't also invested in the best equipment. So I bought the fast bike, the fast wheels and made sure to research what tyres and tubes were going to make a difference to my speed on the day. I also made sure to tick as many of the other boxes as possible – the fastest wetsuit, aero helmet, race kit and more.

In the end, I did miss that slot at my first attempt by only two minutes. But I was satisfied that there was very little more I could have done in the way of kit or preparation to qualify that day. I was beaten by better athletes – not just by better kit.

The onus then rested with me to get fitter, faster and stronger. I ultimately qualified a year later, again racing at Ironman UK, and I put the success that year down to the accumulation of almost eighteen months of consistent training and racing.

In 2016, I decided to make a return to competitive Ironman racing and try to get back to Kona. I again made sure to tick all of the 'marginal gains' boxes. Ironman Mallorca was to be the race where I went to qualify, and I ultimately missed the slot by forty minutes. This, in part, was because when I got off the bike I knew I was already well off target and needed a bit of a miracle on the run. I decided to roll the dice and chase a marathon time that was unrealistic for me given my training. I hoped that I might fluke a fast run split, but of course I just blew up instead.

Even with the best performance I could have hoped for on the day, I would only have moved possibly to within twenty minutes of the last qualifying slot. I was never really in good enough shape to qualify that time. Afterwards, when analysing why I was so far off, one of the thoughts that kept returning to me was how futile and stupid it was to chase all of the small gains when the biggest, most important one, wasn't in place. That missing major gain was the training.

For any of the smaller gains to be effective, I should have been a lot fitter. A fast chain, tyres, or even wheels were never going to bridge a forty- or even twenty-minute gap. So which is it, are marginal gains worth chasing or not? I think they need to be weighed up carefully.

Cost versus potential gains

This is a simple enough equation to work out. If I spend one Euro, Dollar or Pound, how much faster will I go? And is that cost worth the gain? Let's look at one of the big and, in some ways easy, choices first.

Tri bike versus road bike

I guess this isn't really a marginal gain. It's potentially a very big one but it will serve to illustrate the point. It's fairly well accepted that a tri bike is considerably faster than a road bike. A typical gain going from a road bike in a standard road position without tri bars, to a well-fitted tri bike with race wheels, would be between five to ten minutes over 40 km. If you work that out over the 180km of an Ironman, then you are potentially gaining a whopping twenty to forty minutes on the bike leg alone.

For anyone looking to be competitive, then this sort of gain is a no brainer. There are very few athletes who can afford to give up that sort of time on the biggest portion of the race and still be in contention. The downside is that, in cash terms, it's the most expensive one. Even an entry-level tri bike and carbon race wheels might start at €2,500 to €3,000. In a way, it's a relatively easy decision because the benefits are so big. It's just a matter of asking yourself: is the gain worth it and can you afford it?

Diminishing returns

Unfortunately, for those with an unlimited budget (or fortunately for those who don't), doubling or even trebling your bike budget doesn't double or treble your gain on the racecourse. The law of diminishing returns starts to play a part there. As you move from entry-level tri bike and make your way up to the top of the range 'super-bike', the gains gradually become smaller.

The biggest benefit comes from the initial move from a regular road bike and the restricted position (in triathlon terms) it provides, to a tri bike and the more aerodynamic set-up that you can achieve with the different geometry.

There are definitely gains to be made by moving up to a top of the range bike, but those minutes gained start to become very expensive. Those choices then start to become harder to make. If I gain one extra minute over 40 km by spending another €3,000, is that worth it? Of course, this is a purely individual question. Blowing €10,000 on a bike might be one person's weekly discretionary spending, but it might be six months' salary or more to someone else.

Questionable returns

There comes a point where the marginal gains start to become a little bit questionable. I remember asking the current Irish Ironman record holder, Bryan McCrystal, a couple of years ago about his thoughts on switching to oval chain rings. I asked Bryan if he thought they were of any benefit, as he was riding them at the time. His answer was that if they weren't costing him anything in energy *and* there was no risk that they were costing him time *and* there was a potential gain *and* they weren't too expensive, then they were probably worth having.

I think a lot of potential marginal gains fall into this category. These are the small things you can do that may or may not help, but doing them doesn't really come with a penalty. If there is a potential gain and no downside then there isn't any reason not to maximise everything you can.

Risk versus reward

Then we get to the type of marginal gains that need to be looked at relative to their risk. There comes a point when chasing the 'one percenters' is not just an exercise in the ridiculous, but can actually harm your race. At what point is reducing rolling resistance, by going for lighter and lighter tyres with less puncture protection, more of a liability than a gain?

If going from a fast and safe choice of tyre to a marginally faster option, but one without any puncture protection, gains you a potential two to three minutes over an Ironman, is the increased risk of puncturing and losing five to ten minutes at the side of the road fixing a puncture worth it?

If one aero helmet is claimed to be faster than another, but has much less ventilation and your race is in a hot climate, does the potential gain outweigh the risk of overheating, dehydration and ultimately slowing down?

If switching your rear derailleur to oversized pulleys has a claimed saving of two, three or four watts (a saving which might equate to a gain of a couple of minutes over an Ironman), is the resulting degradation in shifting and the risk of dropping a chain as a result worth it?

Does the 'faster' upgrade come with a risk? If so, you need to ask yourself: is the potential reward big enough for me to risk a race result for the promised improvement, especially if it's a once-a-year type of race?

If you are racing sprint and Olympic distance triathlons every week or month, then chasing every possible gain is probably less catastrophic if it doesn't work out. If, however, you only have one shot in a year to take a Kona slot or have that fast Ironman you're chasing, is it worth risking it for a potentially tiny gain?

Nutritional magic bullets

Claimed gains aren't just limited to the bike. I was at Ironman UK a number of years ago and was sucked in by the promises of increased VO2 max and the resulting performance gains I would see if I 'beet-loaded'. At the expo, beetroot juice and concentrated beet shots were being touted as the next nutritional magic bullet.

One ten minute sales pitch later and I was hooked. I bought a full box of a dozen shots two days before the most important race not only of the year, but of my entire racing career up to that point. I bought it on the assurance that if I loaded up in the remaining days before the race I would 'definitely' go faster.

Once we were out of the charged atmosphere of the expo, the craziness started to dissipate and I realised that there was no way that I would risk the preceding eighteen months of training and build-up by trying out a new nutritional supplement in the last couple of days. A supplement that might help, but could also backfire and cost me my race.

In a sport as technical and complex as Ironman, with all of the promises of free speed made by product manufacturers, we need to stop and question not just whether a product will deliver any gain but, more importantly, whether it will harm our race. Marginal gains are all well and good, that is until they become marginal (or even major) losses.

Takeaways

When I weighed up the marginal gains available to me I went for the biggest gain, unless it came with a big risk. For example, I chose the fastest tyres that had a reasonable level of puncture protection available. There were always faster tyres on the market, but I decided that the risk of puncturing, or worse, splitting a tyre, wasn't worth the extra potential gain. The difference between a fast option and the fastest option just wasn't worth the risk in my opinion.

One area where I did maximise the gains available was the bike. It was an area where there wasn't any real risk in going for the fastest one that I could afford.

I have decided not to list the equipment I have used here as it has changed over the years as manufacturers have improved wheels, tyres, wetsuits etc. What I am racing on this year is only relevant now. What I raced on previously doesn't matter and certainly will not in a few years time.

CHAPTER 27

Athletes' favourite sessions

We all have our favourite training sessions. More often than not, when I ask athletes about their favourites, they tend to be the discipline they like most or at which they are strongest.

My favourite run session is the split long run. When I'm in good shape and doing both a morning and evening run with some quality work in them, I cover almost a full marathon in a normal training day. The first time I did that and trained normally the following day it nearly blew my mind.

Almost every marathon I've ever done has left me walking like a geriatric for three days afterwards. Yet by splitting the distance over eight or nine hours, I am only mildly stiff and sore the following day.

Here's what the experts had to say on what their favourite sessions are.

Andy Kinnane

'Definitely the fast-finish long run. It's great for the head as well as the legs. Pushing tempo pace when you already have thirty kilometres in the legs requires willpower. You can't train directly for what the body will feel like in the last ten kilometres of an Ironman marathon, but pushing harder at the end of a long run can help simulate it. Also, for me, I felt I improved my biking when I switched to doing my long bike on Saturday and long run on Sunday. My legs were fresher to allow adaptations to take place and it was also more enjoyable. And maybe training to run on tired bike legs also helps.'

Emma Bilham

When I spent a week riding with Emma she repeatedly said that cycling wasn't training, it was fun. It's a fantastic attitude and way to think about our sport. Fun feels much less like hard work than training sometimes sounds.

'On the bike, I just love heading out into the mountains for three to four hours. Ditch the tri-bars and just ride up a pass or two and screech down the descents. No intervals, just fun.'

'The run ... I'm always scared of tempo sessions but usually end up enjoying the tough ones I can really get my teeth into. I love the satisfaction afterwards. The twenty-one by three minutes is a regular, but there are also more complicated ones where basically you speed up and slow down for the best part of two hours.'

Jocelyn Gardner McCauley

On the run: Five by one mile with three minutes rest, going as fast as possible through all miles.

Swim:
700 swim (7 x 100)
600 swim (6 x 100)
500 swim (5 x 100)
400 swim (4 x 100)
300 swim (3 x 100)
The 100s are all out. The distance swims are at base pace (not recovery).

Bike: Fourteen times one-minute hill repeats. Done at low cadence, all out, down the hill and go again.

Garron Mosley

'The 5,000 m swim set once a week. This was introduced at the beginning of 2016 and has prompted massive improvements over the last two years. Just a swim, no drills but sometimes half will be done with paddles.'

Garron is another fan of split long runs: 'Double run day, a marathon split over two sessions, two hours thirty in the morning and then a forty to forty-five minute run in the late afternoon.'

CHAPTER 28

Turning professional

No, I'm not advocating that you quit your job and spend all day swimming, biking and running (although there are worse ways I could think of spending my time), rather it's an idea that I read about in a book by Stephen Pressfield called *The War of Art*.

The book is actually about writing, but I think a lot of the same principles apply to us and to triathlon. When I was aiming to get to Kona, the more professional I was with my approach, the more likely I was to succeed.

Stephen talks about the traits that differentiate the professional from the amateur. These also happen to be a lot of the things that we all do in our day job where we are actually the professional. He then goes on to show how these things can be applied to how we approach our amateur interests.

1. Professionals show up every day

We all show up in our day jobs. We don't start off being experts or professionals the first day on the job; it takes years of showing up day after day, week after week, until we have our 10,000 hours clocked up.

Training for Ironman is exactly the same. Showing up is more than half the battle. There have been more days than I can remember where I was tired, or slow, or didn't want to ride for whatever reason. But invariably, most of those days end up being the ones that are not only the most satisfying, but are the days that differentiate really successful athletes from the rest. They are also the days that tick so many of the Kona boxes, including consistency, volume, a burning desire to succeed, determination and strength of character. It's quite incredible that such a simple idea can get you almost all the way to Ironman success.

2. Professionals show up no matter what

If you've got a cold, are tired, didn't sleep well last night, are hungover or just really don't want to, you will still show up for work. You'll still clock in do the shift and get the work done. You may not do it perfectly, but done is better than nothing.

Bar serious illness, professionals show up regardless of how they feel. Tired? Fine, slow down and just put in the time. Hungover? Suck it up; that problem is self inflicted. Not in the mood? Nobody said you would love every session.

Ironman is hard. Being good is really hard but anyone who's motivated enough can do it. After all, it's only work. Like I said earlier: no talent is required to sign up.

3. Professionals put in the full day

We don't go home early from work because we aren't in the mood, or because we stub our toe, or because it's cold or raining. The exact same thing applies here. If you're down to do a five-hour ride and there's no physical reason not to do it, then the Garmin file should say you did a five-hour ride. I don't want to hear that you went home early because your mate did, or because it rained, or because you were bored. Go home when the work is done.

4. Professionals are in it for the long haul

We may decide to change jobs next year, but unless we win the lottery we are committed to working for a long time. We don't bitch too much about it. That's just the way life is. We have to work for what we want, and we accept that it often takes a long time.

Ironman is a wonderfully inclusive sport. It doesn't discriminate. It's not like swimming, where physical peculiarities like being very tall, having huge feet and an abnormal wingspan help to make someone like Michael Phelps the best swimmer in the history of the sport. I'm not for one minute diminishing the unbelievable work ethic that got Phelps all of those Olympic medals but, at that level, the physical attributes also make a difference.

Ironman doesn't care if you're a five-feet tall Miranda Carfrae, or a six-foot two Chris McCormac (both of whom are Ironman world champions); it doesn't care if you're a former swimmer or never set foot in the water before starting your journey. If you're willing and physically able to do the work, you can be more successful than you probably imagine. Allow that it will take a long time, but stick with it and the rewards will come.

5. For professionals, success or failure is the difference between eating or not, and being able to pay the rent/mortgage or not

Exactly the same thing applies to us in our professional lives. Our jobs are how we feed our families. For me, getting to Kona was and is an all-consuming passion. Aisling commented when training for her first Ironman, that if you broke her open like a stick of rock you would find a big Mdot running through the middle of her.

When you take a passion or goal as seriously as you take your job, you are much more likely to succeed. That being said, it's very easy to become so obsessed with it that other aspects of your life suffer, which I suppose is exactly the same as with your job. If you allow it to take over your life, your family life and health are likely to suffer as a result. Maybe aiming for a 'balanced obsession' is the best answer.

CHAPTER 29

The vital importance of discipline

Discipline is not a dirty word; it's one of the cornerstones of success that any field is built upon. It's something to be embraced and enjoyed rather than suffered through.

I did my first Ironman in France in 2008. I'd spent years thinking and dreaming about it. I spent about six months training for it, and on lots of those long training rides I anticipated that moment when I would cross the line. I'd read about the effect finishing an Ironman had on people – changing lives and changing people – and I wanted my slice of it. I wanted that moment of euphoric self-discovery.

I crossed the line in Nice and stood there, wobbling unsteadily, as a volunteer put that precious medal around my neck. I waited for the moment of enlightenment. As I stood there and things started to blur and go dark, I wondered if this was it. Was this how it happened? As I crumpled to the floor in a wave of nausea and blackness, I was still waiting.

I was also still waiting for that moment of spiritual awakening as I lay in the medical tent hooked up to an IV drip an hour later. Yet it still eluded me. By the next day, I had very disappointedly given up on it ever arriving. I started to think that all of the stories of Ironman changing lives was either total rubbish or I'd done something wrong. Every so often I looked skyward as if I might see enlightenment drifting above me on a little fluffy white cloud, just waiting to be plucked down from the sky. Unsurprisingly, it didn't.

It was about a week later that it finally happened. I had that moment of self-discovery that I'd been waiting for. I realised that it wasn't the Ironman itself that was life changing (although it was pretty impressive), it was the six months of learning to love the training, the discipline, the routine; of organising my life around building towards and achieving a massive target; of working towards a goal that I once thought impossible. I then realised I loved being an athlete.

Not long after that, my second moment of enlightenment landed. There I was worrying, if I would ever have an epiphany, and then two came along at once – just like waiting for a bus. In managing to do something that I had thought was impossible, I had gained a level of self-belief that I had never before possessed. I realised that I wasn't afraid anymore of dealing with situations in my personal life that, up until then, had seemed impossible to fix. If I could do one thing that had seemed impossible, then there was no reason that I couldn't do more.

Both realisations led to the surprising discovery that I loved the discipline. Being the type of person who always railed against authority and hated being told what to do, I never expected to like such a level of structure and discipline. I guess I always associated routine and discipline with authority and didn't think I'd ever actually enjoy it.

Without fail, the most successful Ironman athletes I know have several things in common: a huge drive, commitment, patience and discipline, to name but a few. They also tend to have very structured and routine lives. Fitting in what is effectively a second job requires a huge level of discipline.

CHAPTER 30

Choose your race carefully

It's getting harder and harder to qualify for Kona. With reduced slots available at races, and more people chasing them, it's becoming increasingly important for most of us that we tick every box possible, starting with training and going right through to equipment choices and set-up. It's also just as important that you choose a race that will reward your strengths and forgive your weaknesses.

My first two qualifications came at Ironman UK, and it wasn't a fluke that I qualified there. It was a conscious decision to pick Bolton, as it very much suited my strengths and forgave my weaknesses.

The course was the first thing my coach considered when choosing a race. Being fairly light and doing well on hills, we wanted a hard hilly bike and run. The swim was the weakest of my three disciplines, so we looked for an easy, flat, wetsuit swim. Ironman UK in Bolton ticked all those boxes and more. The swim was in a flat, calm lake. The bike course was hilly and, almost as importantly, was very technical with lots of turns, junctions and roundabouts that played to my background of both mountain biking and road racing.

The road surface was also more like what I was used to, with a lot of rough chip finish, just like at home in Ireland, which I thought would also be harder on athletes who were more accustomed to smoother, fast surfaces.

Another important consideration was the climate and the weather. It was rarely hot, at least not like it could be at many of the mainland European races, in fact, it was just as likely to be cold, wet and windy: conditions I was used to in training and, as a result, revelled in when racing.

Getting to the race was also on the list of reasons to choose the UK. We could get the ferry and drive there, so the amount of kit we could bring wasn't restricted; I could take spare wheels and could choose which to race on depending on the weather, right up to the last day.

Weather conditions on the day were often completely different to what was forecast when we left home four days before, which was also similar to Ireland. Having all of the kit we could fit into the car meant we were never caught out with the incorrect wheel or clothing choice. We simply brought whatever we thought we might need for every possibility. This isn't really possible or practical if you are flying to a race and are limited with the amount of luggage you can bring.

Picking a destination race because it's somewhere you always wanted to visit is fine if you are looking for that type of race, or holiday experience. For me, if I was trying to qualify, choosing a race was based on where gave me the best chance to do that. Bolton was never going to offer the same type of race experience as somewhere like Nice or Lanzarote, but it gave me a much better opportunity to qualify.

If you're a 60 kg swim-runner who is relatively weak on the bike, then choosing a race with an easy swim and very hard bike course won't allow you to maximise your advantage in the water over weaker swimmers like me. It also puts you at a fairly big disadvantage against the strong, technically proficient bike riders. More importantly, such a hard bike course will leave your legs fried for the run. You would end up not being able to use either of your key strengths.

The time of year is also a very important consideration when choosing a race for many reasons; in my case, we own and run a number of businesses; one of which is seasonal and has very different demands on my time in the winter compared to the summer. Between 2011 and 2013, when I was chasing qualification at Ironman UK and racing at Kona, our main business suffered because I wasn't there as much as I should have been. Racing Ironman UK meant that I was out of the business more than was ideal during the busiest time of the year. When I was there, I was often tired from the huge training load and not functioning very well. That was a cost that we decided we were willing to accept, in order for me to race on the course that we thought suited me best. However, that was never going to be sustainable long term; we now choose our races based as much on the time of year that they fall, as the course and climate that suits. Of course, this is bound to lead to compromises on one or more of our ideal requirements.

It's hard to find a racecourse that suits you perfectly, with an ideal climate and that just happens to fall at the exact time of year that you need, to be able to maximise your training in the lead up to it.

Which of these you decide to give greatest priority to is an individual choice, but I think that the chase for Kona has become so competitive in the last few years that now you almost need to be physically capable of qualifying at any race, regardless of course conditions. There aren't any 'easy' races anymore, in the same way that there is much less chance of qualifying with a roll-down slot than there was five years ago.

Takeaways

Make sure you take into account how the biggest volume of training will fit into your life. If, like me, your job is seasonal, then it's important to allow for this in your planning. If you can't train because you're too busy in work it doesn't matter how well a race suits you, you won't perform to the best of your abilities.

The weather is also a possible consideration, depending on where you live. If you live in Canada or somewhere it's simply too cold to train outdoors for several months of the year, will you be happy sitting on the indoor trainer or running on the treadmill? If the answer is no, then you need to plan your racing around when you can fit in the biggest part of your training.

If you suffer from seasonal allergies that affect your ability to train outdoors, then this is something worth taking into account when planning which race you will do.

If you are aiming to race competitively, you need to list the positives and negatives of a race. You also need to know (and be honest about) your strengths and weaknesses, and then choose your race accordingly.

CHAPTER 31

The importance of supportive relationships

One of the first questions we ask all athletes who come to us for coaching is whether or not they are married or have a significant other in their life. If the answer is yes, we then ask them if the significant other is on board with this wonderful project. And if the answer is still yes, then we ask them if their partner actually knows what that means.

It's very important your partner realises what's involved in the training programme. It's not just about finishing the Ironman or taking a Kona slot or whatever the end goal may be. It's often easy to get someone all excited about the huge goal, but it can be considerably harder to get them on side when you go playing on your bike with your mates for six hours on a Sunday while they change nappies and make the dinner.

This is the crucial part: it doesn't matter how much you want something, it doesn't matter how fired up you are or how willing you are to show up and do the work come rain, hail, sleet or snow, if after three months you come home to find a suitcase on the doorstep after your epic all-day ride, the whole exciting project will come to a screeching, shuddering, catastrophic halt.

When I talk about my training and racing I usually talk about 'we'. This is because I think of Aisling and myself as a team. In terms of my sports, she's more than just my coach. When I'm in heavy training, which might be ten or eleven months a year, a lot of our life is built around accommodating my training, recovery and racing. This takes as much commitment on her part as it does on mine. Admittedly, our coach/athlete relationship is not the normal husband and wife situation as she takes on a much bigger part in my training, but when you're training for Ironman, whether it's for ten or twenty hours a week, remember that it also affects those around you.

A coach or mentor, along with training partners, and even employees can all form part of your support structure. It's a very rare athlete who gets to the start line completely independently. You might do the training, and you might do it all alone, but more often than not you are able to train because of the support of others. This could be financial support from family or sponsors, or support in the form of time from family, a partner, your boss or employees in a business (by allowing you time off to train). It may also be in the form of coaching, teaching or mentoring, or training partners who offer motivation or company during long hard sessions. Whatever form your support structure takes, look after these relationships and pay them back for what they do for you when you can.

For me, the first and most important way to pay back that support is to race hard all the way to the end and never quit, regardless of how well or badly a race is going. I believe this shows all of the people who have made sacrifices to allow me to train and race just how important their support is; it shows them that their sacrifice or contribution is worthwhile and valued.

There's nothing worse than going out of your way to help an athlete get to the start line, only to have them quit because something went wrong and they didn't think they would get the result they hoped for. It gives the message that the support they received in order to help them wasn't all that valuable to them.

If the race isn't important enough that you can't be bothered to finish when something goes wrong, then why should someone else make a sacrifice so you can do it? Why should they value something that you clearly don't?

I find a good supportive network also provides extra motivation when things really start to hurt and it gets hard to keep on pushing. It's easier to push myself to the limit in a race, so that I don't let Aisling down, than it is to quit and have to disappoint her by telling her that I didn't race hard all the way and give it everything I had.

CHAPTER 32

Dealing effectively with race problems

Racing in the real world means learning to deal with adversity and injustice, bad weather, bad luck and bad calls by the referee. The very best athletes I know learnt very early on in their racing careers that railing against an injustice (either real or imagined) does nothing except remove their focus from the task at hand and waste valuable energy.

Look at the example of professional athlete, Patrick Lange, racing in Kona in 2016. He entered the second transition in twenty-second position after receiving a five-minute penalty on the bike. He would probably have been excused if he just accepted where he was and stopped fighting. Instead, he started the run like his race was still on track and moved steadily up through the field, making it all the way to third and claiming Mark Allen's Kona run course record in the process.

Lange didn't bitch and moan about the injustice of the penalty he received on the bike, or get distracted by what might have been. Even after the race, in an interview, he accepted it as being his mistake and was delighted with what he had achieved.

The best athletes understand that having problems, or a bad stretch, is normal in a race that lasts for eight, nine or ten hours.

One of the most important lessons I ever learnt was from Aisling when she said that no matter what problems you encounter in a race, you must push as hard as if you were chasing a victory or a paycheck.

In a small, local, Olympic distance race a number of years ago I showed up without the correct preparation. I don't mean physically, because I was in good shape and thought I'd be competitive, rather I didn't take the race seriously as it was only a small local event. I showed up with my fancy tri bike, deep section front wheel and rear disc wheel, aero helmet and aero bottle on the bike. That makes it sound like I was all prepped and ready to go.

The problem was that, although the weather was good when we left home on Friday afternoon, there was a storm due to land on Saturday. Not a bad enough storm to jeopardise the race but one that brought big winds. I woke to the stormy conditions and realised my mistake. I hadn't brought my spare wheels, so I had to ride the 90 mm deep front and the disc wheel with gusts hitting 70 kph and more.

On the bike, I almost came off a couple of times riding past gaps in hedges, and I eventually spent almost the entire ride on the bull bars, losing places to athletes that I normally beat easily; these were athletes who had made the correct equipment choice for the day.

I was so pissed off, both with myself and the world in general, that by the time I got back to T2, I threw a tantrum the whole way through transition. I stamped around like a four-year-old. When Aisling saw me so far down the field and walking through transition she was initially worried that I'd crashed or was injured. When she realised I was just throwing a tantrum, she shouted at me to get my act together because I was still in a race.

I realised how stupid I looked and how childishly I was acting and started to run. I quickly got back into race mode and started picking off people ahead of me. I went on to have my fastest run over the distance, probably due to the very easy bike. But it taught me that no matter what problems we encounter, we can salvage something from a race.

Aisling, for the first time ever, was really pissed with me. I realised that the result didn't matter to her, only the effort. She didn't care if I won my age group or came in last, only that I raced honestly, which meant pushing hard all the way to the end, without quitting.

She taught me that day that a result isn't within our control, only our effort. We can't base our satisfaction with our racing on our result. For most of us, more often than not, our result will be lower than we expect, but by pushing hard all the way to the end regardless of placing or problems, we can still have pride in our performance.

The other thing I realised was how invested Aisling was in my racing. I realised for the first time that by giving up, I was letting her down. That hurt more than the poor placing in the race. I've finished races disappointed with the result, but nothing stings like the feeling that I didn't race honestly, or that I quit before the end and let Aisling down.

CHAPTER 33

Talent should be mental, rather than physical

You may have noticed that I haven't spoken much about talent. That's because I think that given enough time, and with enough training, almost anyone can get to Kona. The really difficult part of Kona is getting the correct combination of time and training.

Most people who attempt to qualify for Kona don't appreciate just how long it will take, how slowly progress comes and how hard it is to keep going when it looks like you will never get there.

If you're on the edge of qualifying, like I was in 2011, and just can't seem to make it to that last couple of places, it can be difficult to start all over again and dedicate another six or twelve months to a goal that might start to seem impossible, especially if it has taken several years to get that close already.

Maybe there is a talent that's required, but it is a mental, and not a physical one. Maybe it's just the stubbornness to keep on trying until you succeed. I know a lot of athletes who've got themselves up into the top twenty, or even the top ten, of their age group a number of times, but never broke through to that last level to take a Kona slot.

I've mentioned Alan Couzens already in this book, and from his two decades in the sport as a coach, he believes that, given enough training pretty much anyone can get to Kona. The problem really lies in living the reality that he outlines: he has calculated the training hours of his athletes over the years – both those who qualify and those who don't – and says it's as simple as hitting a number.

Alan believes that qualifying currently takes an average of 800 to 1,000 hours of training a year. Allowing for a couple of weeks off after Kona, and another one after a qualifying race, and maybe three to four reduced weeks allowing for tapering for those two races, that means that to qualify athletes need to train an average of seventeen to twenty one hours a week for the rest of the year.

If they do a six or seven-hour training day at the weekend, and maybe another four- to five-hour day during the week, that leaves them with two to three hours a day training for the other three days. That's also not allowing for any easy weeks.

The 'talent' required to get to Kona is probably better described as the ability to do that much training without breaking down.

The key is to have the desire and drive to actually do the work and also to create a life that allows you fit it all in.

Also, by Rob Cummins

Chasing Kona

Available at Amazon as an ebook or paperback

<u>Chapter 1</u>

Bolton – August 2011

My legs hurt. My neck and back both ache. My backside is in a lot of discomfort.

I shift in the saddle as I slide forward, dropping down two gears and spinning my legs faster, trying to relax the muscles that are overworking and desperately trying to get some relief from the pain. I'm trying to hold my average speed constant, something that is becoming increasingly difficult to do. It's getting harder to keep pushing as I tire. I think of my coach back at home watching the results popping up live online and I wonder what he's thinking. When we started working together he didn't believe I could do this and only took me on as a client reluctantly. It's been one of the things that has kept me motivated over the last four months; the thought that I'd prove him wrong. I shift back up a gear. I accelerate. I hold on to the hurt. I won't slow down. I won't fail. I look ahead and see someone in the distance and focus on them.

I remember Aisling's advice to focus on the next one and go after him, then the next and the next. Her exact words were to 'hunt those motherfuckers down'. I can hear her now in my mind telling me to push, to stretch myself – to reach further than I believe possible. And that makes me shift another gear and push even harder. I look up the road and work out the time gap to the next athlete. He's just over one minute ahead. The road rises a little and I shift up a couple of gears and get up out of the saddle, stretching my back and giving my aching legs something else to shout about. I settle into a rhythm on the climb, the bike swaying in time with my pedal stroke. My world shrinks down to just the spot ahead of my front wheel and for a while the pain fades into the background. I shift gear again and accelerate. My legs protest slightly then decide they will cooperate and settle. And then I've found that sweet spot below my threshold that I feel I could hold on to all day. It seems like I'm dancing. I feel light on the pedals. For a moment it's effortless. I look ahead and I'm surprised to see that rider is now right in front of me. I've closed the gap quickly. I pull out and ride by him. He's labouring on the short hill and I realise that he's blown his lights. He's cooked. Probably started too fast and now he's paying the price. I flick the fingers of my left hand in greeting as I overtake. He doesn't respond. He's inside his own head and doesn't seem aware of me.

I crest the rise and drop gingerly back into the saddle, squirming and shifting around to find some position that doesn't hurt. There isn't one, so I push on regardless. The pain in my legs and everywhere else is back. The brief respite while I was out of the saddle is over and it's back to business. Another rider is visible in the distance and again I remember Aisling's words 'hunt that motherfucker down'. It's become a mantra playing over and over in my head, distracting me from the pain, giving me another focus and he comes closer to me. I drop another gear and accelerate hard to make the pass. I want to make sure he doesn't try to follow and a part of me wants to demoralise him. No not demoralise, destroy. I want to make sure that there's no chance that he even tries to race me. I want him to feel so weak that he quits. I want to crush him.

Outside of racing and off the bike I'm not like this, and I never admit to having these feelings except to one or two people. I'm afraid that I'll be called an arsehole;I'll be judged for it and that people will think that this is my usual mind-set. But right now I'm looking up the road for the next target. It takes a couple of minutes but I see someone in the distance. It looks like a woman. She must be one of the pros. I've passed a couple of female professionals so far, which is the only indication that I'm near the front end of the field and the fact that the field has thinned out considerably. The riders I'm catching are further and further apart as I move through.

I glance down to check my average speed and it looks good. I'm almost on target and haven't slowed down at all in the second half of the race. I take encouragement from this fact and push again, despite the increasingly loud protests from my legs. I round a corner and come upon a female rider. She's slowed a bit and as I ride past I look at the name on her number and realise that it's Desiree Flicker. She was in the pre-race media as being the favourite to win the women's pro race. I feel a huge swell of emotion and excitement rising inside me. Initially I try to suppress it, before giving in and embracing it. If I've just passed the favourite in the women's race then I'm probably much closer to the front of the field than I had thought. It's the first time that I really start to believe that I can do this and the feelings of excitement, mixed with relief, are bursting within me.

The pain suddenly disappears and I push harder. I'm riding on a huge wave of emotion. I use the feelings as fuel and push harder. There's not far to go now and as I rise out of the saddle to start the short rise to the turn-off point, I again feel like I'm dancing and have to hold myself back a little. There's a big crowd at the turn-off point and I get a huge cheer when they realise that I'm almost finished and not going out to start another lap. The shouting and cheering lifts me further and I look around and smile at them. I try to burn as much of this into my memory and try to store the emotions to fire me up for the marathon still to come.

It's only a couple of kilometres to the second transition and the end of the bike leg and I ride in fast. The crowd is a little smaller here but the noise is fantastic. I've slipped my feet out of the bike shoes and am pedalling with my feet on top of them. I turn the last corner and see the dismount line some 50m ahead. I don't slow down and the marshals are getting a little worried that I might not stop. They wave and shout, pointing at the white line on the ground. In one fluid and well practised move I rise out of the saddle, swing my right leg over the bike and only a couple of feet before the line I drop off the other pedal at over 20 kph and land at a run just like I've done in countless short course races.

My legs scream in disbelief at the stupidity of this idea and simply refuse to cooperate. I almost land on my face right there in front of everyone but somehow manage to stay upright and turn right into transition. I'm shocked to see that it's almost empty, which means I'm right up at the front of the field. In my mind I'd visualised racing and crossing the line and qualifying many times in training, but I somehow had overlooked the fact that to be competitive in my age group would mean being competitive overall. It's one of those really obvious things that I should have been expecting, but I was shocked by it. I guess a big part a part of me never really believed it would happen. It hits me again and I start to believe I can race at this level. I'm doing it, I'm actually doing it! The thought keeps going round in my head. I've dreamed of this for years but it's one thing having a dream. It's another actually making it happen. Until this precise moment, I never really believed it was possible.

I hand off my bike and marvel once more at all the empty racks. My legs still aren't working properly though and it's a lumpy, uncoordinated run through transition. I enter the hall where our run bags are lined up on the floor where we left them. I run straight to mine, but I'm directed over to the side of the hall to a row of benches. I sit down heavily. I sort of collapse really, my quads screaming in protest.

I lean over to pull on my shoes and my hamstring goes into the most awful cramp. My leg shoots out in front of me and for the second time in a matter of minutes I almost land face down. I twist and try to stretch out. One of the marshals starts coming over towards me to see if I'm alright and I wave her off. The cramp subsides but I still haven't got my shoe on and I'm afraid that if I try again it will spasm out of control, landing me on the floor scrabbling around like an upended beetle. The clock is ticking and the urgency is building. My stomach is tightening into a hard ball of tension. I reach down as quickly as I can, bending my leg at the same time. I can feel the muscle pulling into a savage cramp again and I pull my shoe on viciously and straighten my leg, stretching it out and grimacing against the pain of the partially cramping hamstring. I reach into my bag, grabbing my hat and run belt. The marshal takes my bag and tells me to go. I hobble into a shambling run out the door. In all, my transition time was one minute forty seconds. It felt like five times that.

It's a downhill start out of transition and I concentrate on small fast steps. I'm trying to get my legs working. There's very little spectator support out here and I take the time to settle myself and try to find a rhythm. I pull on my hat as I run and fasten my run belt around my waist, adjusting it until it sits low on my hips and doesn't bounce.

I have a pacing plan that I'm determined to stick to rigidly. I'm aiming on running easy for the first 10k, then build to as fast a cruise as I can maintain for the middle 20k section, then hang on for dear life for the last 12k. I'm reminded of a quote I heard somewhere that goes 'If you want to make God laugh, tell him about your plans.' I decide to keep them to myself for the moment. Ais and the coach both warned me several times, I should not start too fast, regardless of how good I'm feeling. I check my Garmin and the first kilometre is fast – a little too fast – so I back off. It feels easy and I settle into a groove almost immediately. I check my Garmin again and the second kilometre is still too fast. I back off a bit more and this pace is starting to feel slow. I'm getting that slightly panicked feeling again in my stomach. I look over my shoulder feeling like I'm going so slowly that I must be caught by the whole field. I expect to see a stampede of tall, fit, tanned triathletes bearing down on me, but there's only a couple of guys strung out along the road. I turn back to the task at hand and start to look ahead, thinking about 'hunting those motherfuckers down'.

I feel like I'm straining against an invisible leash. My legs saying 'fuck it let's go', my head saying 'don't be a clown'. I pass the three-kilometre marker. My legs have settled after the cycling and every part of me is grateful to be upright and not crouched down over my tri-bars. I shake my arms, working out the stiffness from the bike and my Garmin beeps to tell me I've done another kilometre. That was quick, I think. My pace is now bang on target but it still feels way too easy. I tell myself to have patience, but the fear of being caught is building inside me again. I look over my shoulder, but there's still no one close to me. As I turn and look ahead I realise I'm gaining on the guy in front. I check my pace again and I'm still on target. Beep. The Garmin tells me that's another kilometre done. I feel like I'm gliding, it feels so easy and I want so badly to stride out and push the pace. I still feel like I'm straining on an imaginary leash.

I'm running alongside a canal and there are no spectators here – just the runner up ahead and one quite a bit behind. The sun is out and I can taste the salt from hours of sweat on my lips. The Garmin beeps again, six kilometres. I look down to be sure. It only feels like seconds since the last one. I look ahead and now the runner in front is only a couple of metres ahead. I pick up my pace just a little. Just to make the pass I tell myself, then I'll slow back down. God it feels good to open it up. I glide by and, as I pass, I pat him on the back and offer a word of encouragement. He tells me I'm flying and to keep it up. I should slow back down to my target pace but I don't. It feels too good, so I just push on. It's completely effortless. I cruise the length of the canal loving the feeling of the sun on my skin and the silence. The faster pace has my breathing a little quicker at first but, as I've sometimes found, the body adapts to the workload after a couple of minutes.

Sure enough everything settles again. My breathing slows and I'm holding the faster pace with what seems like no greater effort than before. I reach the end of the canal section and there's a steep hill up to the main part of the course. I love running hills and normally hit the gas hard, pushing right up to the red line and holding it there before backing off over the crest and recovering on the downhill. I don't think that will work in an Ironman marathon. At least, I don't have the nerve to test the theory so I slow right down. Just as I'm reaching the halfway point of the hill a guy comes flying past me. 'Jesus he looks strong', I think to myself and almost give in to the urge to chase. I tell myself that he's either going too hard, in which case he'll blow up and I'll catch him or he's just faster than me, in which case I won't. Either way, I just have to run my own race. As it turns out, I see him again in about fifteen minutes, vomiting at the side of the road.

I crest the hill and come onto the lapped part of the run course. There are more spectators here, but the course itself is almost empty. I still can't believe that I'm up here with the leading athletes. It was exactly as I had dreamed on all of those long bike rides and runs, when I had endless hours to imagine what it would feel like. I never imagined it would feel like this. Never in my wildest dreams did I think I would run like this. I tell myself to enjoy it while I can.

I see an Irish flag up ahead and I accelerate a little, the excitement driving me on. I'm vaguely aware somewhere in the back of my mind that I might be going too fast, but then I pass the Irish fans and they recognise the Wheelworx kit and give me a big shout. It gives me a huge lift and I pick up the pace a little more, feeling incredible. I'm cruising, feeling like I can do this all day, and although it isn't quite as effortless as it has been, it's very comfortable and still the Garmin keeps beeping telling me I've done another kilometre, and again I'm surprised at how quickly it happens and I also keep ignoring the voice in the back of my head that's telling me I might be going too fast. I had practised my nutrition in training and so far it has been working perfectly. I drop down the hill into Bolton city centre for the first time and the crowds and the noise are building...

Chasing Kona is available at Amazon as an ebook or paperback.

Made in the USA
Middletown, DE
27 July 2023

35814532R00130